Philosophy of Religion for AS Level

Philosophy of Religion for AS Level

Michael B. Wilkinson

&

Hugh N. Campbell

continuum

Published by Continuum

The Tower Building   80 Maiden Lane
11 York Road   Suite 704
London   New York
SE1 7NX   NY 10038

www.continuumbooks.com

First published 2009
Reprinted 2009

British Library Cataloguing-in-Publication Data
A catalogue record for this book is available from the British Library.

ISBN-13: PB: 978–1–8470–6540–7
ISBN-10: PB: 1–8470–6540–6

Typeset by RefineCatch Limited, Bungay, Suffolk
Printed and bound in Great Britain by
MPG Books Ltd, Bodmin, Cornwall

Contents

Introduction

No new book should be produced without a very good justification. For us, the motivation was straightforward – the wish to help as many students as possible, based on our extensive experience as examiners, not merely marking scripts, but also in setting papers and overseeing their marking. We receive many enquiries about why scripts have been marked in a particular way, why students expected to do well have done less than expected, but also enquiries on the interpretations of aspects of the subject. Our intention is partly to answer some of those needs, but there is more than this.

We have a duty to the subject we love. There is more to that than simply passing exams. We believe in the subject, we think it touches on some of the deepest questions of mankind, and we want to share that enthusiasm. Sometimes textbooks become lists of facts to be learned – they become dominated by the bullet-point approach. These are valuable tools to *learning* about Philosophy, but they are not the secret of *being* a philosopher. For the examination, we have provided the points in skeleton notes as an appendix to the text. But Philosophy is more than as well as other than just that.

To engage in Philosophy is to take ideas and watch them dance; and then, when ready, to join in the dance. The great philosophers do not simply lay out arguments, and want them to be learned. They are involved in conversation – they set out ideas for our response, sometimes anticipating our objections, sometimes ignoring them, occasionally paying them too little attention. The reader engages in a conversation, dances with the flow of ideas. And ideas are developed – they are not bullet points or absolutes like the bones in the body or the stars in the Pleiades. For this reason, we have determined to write a book which gives something of the flavour of those conversations, with space for ideas to dance. That is why we have chosen an essentially narrative approach, but with clear indications of the arguments to be learned. This is a book to be read and thought about and, when it is right to do so, disputed. For this reason we have not cluttered the text with marginal boxes and activities. These have value but break the flow. We have sought a clean, uncluttered text, seeking also to show in our prose how complex ideas might be clearly expressed. It is for you to judge whether we have succeeded.

A key concern has been to avoid errors which have crept into the work of others. In one well-known text, we detected 29 factual errors in the first 11 pages on the Philosophy of Religion. Many of the errors come from the Chinese whispers effects of reinterpretations of secondary texts themselves taken from secondary texts. As far as we have been able, we have always returned to primary texts. All Latin texts given have been freshly translated by us. One of the results has been what we hope are improved interpretations, such as those of Irenaeus, St Anselm and St Thomas Aquinas. But our account of modern writers, such as Behe, has been based on careful reading of their work. Further, we have been careful to provide adequate background and context to our descriptions of theories. Although the validity of arguments is independent of context, knowing the predominant currents of thought which shaped them is an invaluable tool for interpretation. An underlying theme of the book is the relationship of philosophical, scientific and religious thought. The new specifications emphasize the significance of science. In this, and overall, we have kept our account close to the specifications. But we have reflected the wish of QCA to encourage students to think beyond the narrow confines of the specification. We have eschewed the casual approach which says, 'you might like to read x for yourself'. Instead, we have looked at wider arguments, clearly labelled where found as 'Stretch and Challenge'.

Many people have contributed, consciously or otherwise, to this book. Special thanks are owed to Haaris Naqvi of Continuum – without his encouragement, wisdom and enthusiasm, this would not exist. Thanks too to John Gwinnell, who introduced us, to John Frye, our mentor, to teachers and fellow-examiners with whom the conversation – and the dance – continue. A special debt is owed to distinguished philosophers who have invited us to join their discussions, notably Patrick Sherry, Michael Durrant, Mark Wynn and Anthony O'Hear among the living, and Dewi Phillips, Czesław Lejewski, John Fitzgerald and Desmond Paul Henry who are no longer with us. Friendship makes so much possible – our friends and colleagues have been steadfast in support. We would also like to thank Frank Morris and Michael O'Duffin from the Science faculty at St Aloysius College for their assiduous checking of the accuracy of the science used in the book. Imelda and Tina are constant in support; to demands made on our time and their patience by our examining have been added the spectacle of our writing. Above all, our thanks to students past, present, and future – to them we dedicate this book.

Michael Wilkinson
Hugh Campbell

Preparing for the Examination

After each chapter you will find an exercise in the format prescribed for the examination. Each question has two parts. Part a) is worth 25 marks, Part b) 10 marks. This immediately should be used as a guide to how much writing is required. Examiners often find carelessness about relative lengths of answers – and remember that if you do not answer a question at all, no marks are awarded. Examiners are not allowed to compensate if a candidate wrote one good answer but missed the other parts of the paper. If you achieved an excellent answer to one part of the question, worth 25 marks, but answered nothing else, 25 would be the maximum you could receive for the paper as a whole.

Examiners begin marking with one clear idea in their minds: 'Has this candidate answered the question set?' If you do not, however good the material used, you will not achieve much. Many people wrongly think that examinations test how much you know. They do not. They test *whether you can answer the question*. Of course, in answering the question you need accurate information to support the answer, but accurate information by itself does not guarantee good marks. An easy way to think of this is to imagine someone in London asking you the way to St Pancras Station as he has a train to catch. Now, St Pancras is an architectural wonder, one of the greatest British stations, home to Eurostar and the longest champagne bar in the world, with a statue of Sir John Betjeman, etc., etc. But if you told your questioner all that, you would not have given him the information he requested – and he would have missed his train. No marks to you.

So, focus carefully on what you are asked to do. Further advice will be given on this in some of the exercises. Here we will concentrate on the question format.

Part a)

This, for 25 marks, will always ask you to explain or describe a given theory or theories. The emphasis of this question is factual – do you know? But, notice that the examiner tests your knowledge, and the way to know whether someone understands something is to see whether she can *explain* it. The key here is to think about for whom you are writing – always write with a clear picture of the audience. Now, the examiner may have studied the subject for forty years, but as an examiner, he adopts the position of a generally intelligent reader. If he read your account as a well-read layman, would he understand your account, or would he need answers to things that you have not mentioned? Have you given clear examples to show your understanding? It is often said that the best way to learn a subject is to have to teach it – listen to yourself explaining the idea. A good way to revise for this examination is to find a willing friend who has not studied it and to answer her questions as you try to explain something like the Ontological Argument.

Familiarize yourself with the mark scheme for this examination. For Part a) the scheme is this:

Mark Band	Mark	Description
0	0	Absent/no relevant material
1	1–5	Almost completely ignores the question • Little relevant material • Some concepts inaccurate • Shows little knowledge of technical terms Communication: often unclear or disorganized
2	6–10	Focuses on the general topic rather than directly on the question • Knowledge limited and partly accurate • Limited understanding • Selection often inappropriate • Limited use of technical terms Community: some clarity and organization
3	11–15	Satisfactory attempt to address the question • Some accurate knowledge • Appropriate understanding • Some successful selection of material • Some accurate use of technical terms Communication: some clarity and organization

Mark Band	Mark	Description
4	16–20	A good attempt to address the question • Accurate knowledge • Good understanding • Good selection of material • Technical terms mostly accurate Communication: generally clear and organized
5	21–25	An excellent attempt to address the question showing understanding and engagement with the material • Very high level of ability to select and deploy relevant information • Accurate use of technical terms Communication: answer is well constructed and organized

Notice here how important it is to answer the question. The heading to each box sets the maximum band you can achieve. If you wrote everything you knew about the Ontological Argument, however accurate, if the question was 'Describe the Ontological Argument of Descartes', then you would only have written about the general area – the question was specific to one version and one only. Picking just the Ontological Argument as a whole would put you in Level 2 – General topic.

We suggest that you use the grid to reflect critically on every piece of writing you do. This will give you essential and invaluable practice. Notice also the importance of taking care to write accurate English and to use technical terms with precision.

Part b)

In this question you are asked to reach a judgement, to explain, evaluate or to discuss. Sometimes there will be a quotation. If you are asked to discuss or evaluate something, you are being asked whether you believe it is true, and why. Simply to say 'I believe . . .' is not philosophical – philosophers insist always on giving reasons.

It is important to note here that part of the concern of examiners is that you have *thought* about the issues as you have worked your way through the course. You cannot hope in the few minutes of the examination to develop your ideas from scratch in the examination room. As you work, and as you revise, never just *learn* arguments. *Think* about them. Consider which convince you, and which do not, and ask yourself *why* you are convinced. The best candidates have always thought through the issues. Weaker ones have learned them, but not made them part of their intellectual life. Work on reaching a conclusion, with reasons, showing awareness of alternative views and why you reject them.

The mark scheme for this part is:

Mark Band	Mark	Description
0	0	Absent/no argument
1	1–2	Very little argument or justification of viewpoint • Little or no successful analysis Communication: often unclear or disorganized
2	3–4	An attempt to sustain an argument and justify a viewpoint • Some analysis, but not successful • Views asserted but not successfully justified Communication: some clarity and organization
3	5–6	The argument is sustained and justified • Some successful analysis which may be implicit Communication: some clarity and organization
4	7–8	A good attempt at using evidence to sustain an argument • Some successful and clear analysis • Might put more than one point of view Communication: generally clear and organized
5	9–10	An excellent attempt which uses a range of evidence to sustain an argument • Comprehends the demands of the question • Shows understanding and critical analysis of different viewpoints Communication: answer is well constructed and organized

Notice again that the levels are directed to how well you create an argument *which answers the question*. Notice also how those most highly rewarded are not those who just *put* different points of view they have learned. The best have demonstrated their own understanding and thoughtfulness.

Doing well in the examination is always a matter of doing the simple things well. Ask always, 'What precisely am I asked to do? What is the precise instruction?' Obey that, using appropriate knowledge, and you cannot fail.

Timeline

Pythagoras (fl.530 BC)

Heraclitus (c. sixth century BC)

Parmenides (c.520–c.450 BC)

Socrates (469–399 BC)

Plato (427–347 BC)

Aristotle (384–322 BC)

Cicero (106–43 BC)

Jesus Christ (c.4 BC–c.29 AD)

St Paul (??–AD 64/67)

St Irenaeus (c.130–c.202)

Origen (c.185–254)

Plotinus (205–c.269)

Porphyry (c.232–c.305)

St Augustine of Hippo (354–430)

Boethius (c.480–524)

Al-Kindi (c.801–866)

Al-Farabi (870–950)

Avicenna (Ibn Sina) (980–1037)

St Anselm of Canterbury (1033–1109)

Al-Ghazali (1058/9–1111)

Abelard (1079–1142)

Averröes (1126–1198)

Moses Maimonides (1124–1198)

St Albertus Magnus (St Albert the Great) (c.1200–1280)

St Bonaventure (1221–1274)

St Thomas Aquinas (1224/5–1274)

William of Ockham (c.1285–c.1349)

Erasmus of Rotterdam (1465–1536)

Martin Luther (1483–1536)

John Calvin (1509–1564)

Archbishop James Ussher (1581–1656)

Hugo Grotius (1583–1645)

Thomas Hobbes (1588–1679)

René Descartes (1596–1650)

Baruch Spinoza (1632–1677)

John Locke (1632–1704)

Sir Isaac Newton (1642–1727)

Gottfried Leibniz (1646–1716)

George Berkeley (1685–1753)

David Hume (1711–1776)

Immanuel Kant (1724–1804)

William Paley (1743–1805)

Jeremy Bentham (1748–1832)

Georg Hegel (1770–1831)

John Henry, Cardinal Newman (1801–1890)

John Stuart Mill (1806–1873)

Charles Darwin (1809–1882)

Philip Gosse (1810–1888)

Søren Kierkegaard (1813–1855)

Karl Marx (1818–1883)

Frederick Temple, Archbishop of Canterbury (1821–1902)

Franz Brentano (1838–1917)

William James (1842–1910)

Friedrich Nietzsche (1844–1900)

Gottlob Frege (1848–1925)

Sir James Frazer (1854–1941)

Sigmund Freud (1856–1939)

Alfred North Whitehead (1861–1947)

Bertrand Russell (1872–1970)

Jan Łukasiewicz (1878–1956)

Pierre Teilhard de Chardin (1881–1955)

Archbishop William Temple (1881–1944)

Moritz Schlick (1882–1936)

Tadeusz Kotarbinski (1886–1981)

Paul Tillich (1886–1965)

Martin Heidegger (1889–1976)

Ludwig von Wittgenstein (1889–1951)

Rudolf Carnap (1891–1970)

Charles Hartshorne (1897–2000)

Gilbert Ryle (1900–1976)

Karl Popper (1902–1994)

Dorothy Emmet (1904–2000)

Karl Rahner (1904–1984)

Jean-Paul Sartre (1905–1980)

F. C. Copleston (1907–1994)

A. J. Ayer (1910–1989)

Norman Malcolm (1911–1990)

Czesław Lejewski (1913–2001)

Peter Geach (1916–)

J. L. Mackie (1917–1981)

Basil Mitchell (1917–)

R. M. Hare (1919–2002)

John Hick (1922–)

Antony Flew (1923–)

Maurice Wiles (1923–2005)

Michael Dummett (1925–)

Herbert McCabe (1926–2001)

John Polkinghorne (1930–)

Alvin Plantinga (1932–)

Don Cupitt (1934–)

Dewi Zephaniah Phillips (1934–2006)

Richard Swinburne (1934–)

Robert Nozick (1938–2002)

Keith Ward (1938–)

Peter Atkins (1940–)

Michael Ruse (1940–)

Richard Dawkins (1941–)

Peter van Inwagen (1942–)

Peter Vardy (1945–)

Eberhard Herrman (1946–)

Michael Behe (1952–)

Alister McGrath (1953–)

Philosophy – The Basics

Introduction

Philosophy of Religion can seem daunting in its use of sometimes technical language. The purpose of this chapter is to provide some basic concepts used in the subject. It is very unlikely that after one reading you will remember all these terms, so remember to turn back to this chapter frequently as you work through the remainder of the book.

What you learn here should have value to you not only in this subject but across all your learning and in the development of your own ideas.

What Philosophy Is

Ask any philosopher to explain this, and you will receive many opinions. However, the disagreement between philosophers tends to be about what the task of philosophy ought to be, or about the main questions that should be considered, rather than the descriptions which should be given to the main branches. So, a philosopher might wonder whether it is possible to do significant work in a particular branch of the discipline, such as Ethics, but would be unlikely to dispute what Ethics broadly means, while probably disputing every other question about it.

So what do philosophers do? In brief, they think about fundamental questions. This does not mean they simply offer theories as answers to the questions. They spend much of their time pondering whether a question is the right one, as well as the implications of it.

Take an apparently straightforward case – the question that is being asked in this book – *Does God exist?* Think about this for a moment, just as a question. What does it mean to ask the question? If I ask: 'Does the Loch Ness Monster exist?' I am asking something like 'Is there in the world a being which has certain characteristics and lives in Loch Ness?' In other words, I am asking if there is a Loch Ness Monster as a real animal, like other real animals – lions, guinea pigs or gerbils. But if I ask whether God exists, I am not asking whether there is an object in the world like other things in the world. If God exists, his existence is not like that of an animal or a rock. God is not a being like anything else, and, if he exists, his existence is not like the existence of anything else. Because God is not like anything else, the question of his existence is not like any other sort of question about what exists.

We might go further and point out several kinds of subordinate question. What would be the being of God (we cannot easily ask what *kind* of thing God is, as he would be like nothing else – there would be no other kind of God)? What would it be to prove that God exists? A fisherman might net the Loch Ness Monster, but God is not a being to be caught like that. When might I have enough evidence of God? What kind of evidence could there be, and what would be enough? And so on . . . You may think of many more examples of your own.

The questions so far have really been of two kinds: one about the nature of the being of God, the other about how we know, what would count as knowledge of God, what would count as proof. People often say that they *believe* in God; some may even say that they *know* God exists. When is it reasonable to have a belief (I may have unreasonable beliefs, after all)? What is the point at which I can move from belief to knowledge? These are some key questions for this chapter.

Three Branches of Philosophy

Philosophy has many branches, such as Ethics, Aesthetics, Political Philosophy and many others. Anything that can be the subject of thought can have a philosophical discipline accompanying it – so long as we continue as a question-asking species, there will be Philosophy.

For Philosophy of Religion, three wide disciplines continually recur – *Metaphysics*, *Epistemology* (*Theory of Knowledge*) and *Logic*.

Metaphysics

This branch of Philosophy received its name when Aristotle's pupils were editing his courses of lectures after his death. They had just finished editing the notes about how things move and change, which, sensibly, they called *The Physics*. Then they were left with a course for which they had no name, so they called it *The Metaphysics*, which meant simply 'beyond the Physics'.

Metaphysics is sometimes understood to deal simply with transcendent matters – that is, to do with things beyond our normal experience. But to think of it in this way would be an error. The central metaphysical question is: *What exists?* So, to ask whether material objects, such as tables or gerbils, exist, is as much a metaphysical question as whether God exists or souls exist.

Traditionally, metaphysical theories are divided into two kinds:

Cosmological – that is, theories of the whole of being, such as found in the work of Plato or Hegel;

Ontological – that is, theories of whether things of this or that kind exist, without making a grand theory of everything. So, for example, to ask whether souls exist is an ontological question, as it leaves entirely open questions about what other kinds of things there might be.

Epistemology

This is sometimes referred to as **Theory of Knowledge**. It is about what we can be said to know – so it involves questions such as my knowledge of the external world or other minds, but also questions about the differences between knowledge and belief, which are obviously directly relevant to religious belief. Epistemology asks questions such as what would count as evidence, and such as what would be sufficient evidence to justify the existence of God – or, indeed, the Loch Ness Monster. Questions of knowledge can often interweave with those of metaphysics, which, after all, concerns what might exist to be known. (It is perhaps worth mentioning that some twentieth-century philosophers, such as A. J. Ayer, argued that metaphysics was meaningless and attempted to construct epistemology without any commitment to the existence of objects, while others, like Czesław Lejewski, argued that connection with real objects was essential to meaning and knowledge.)

An essential division of knowledge is that between the *a priori* and the *a posteriori*.

A priori

This refers to knowledge which is not dependent on sense experience, but on the meaning of words. For example, to say 'a square has four sides' is true and I can know it to be true provided I know the meanings of all the words in the sentence. A sentence of this sort is called a *tautology*, which simply means that the meaning of the predicate ('has four sides' – this is the bit of the sentence which describes the subject) is an essential part of the meaning of the subject ('A square' – what the sentence is about).

Notice that the meaning is not dependent on sense experience. This can be confusing, but becomes clearer if we think back to learning arithmetic when we were young. We learn through sense experience, perhaps by counting bricks or cherries, that two bricks and two bricks make four bricks, or that two cherries and two cherries make four cherries. That is the psychological fact of how we learn that $2 + 2 = 4$. But we do not wake up in the night wondering whether two bricks and two bricks still make four bricks – once we can see the truth of $2 + 2 = 4$, we do not need to check it again, while other types of sentence ('There are fairies at the bottom of my garden') would need to be checked by looking to see whether it was still true.

There is philosophical disagreement about what can be known *a priori*. The key question is whether there are any truths beyond tautologies that can be known this way. Descartes famously attempted to prove his own existence this way, when he wrote '*Cogito ergo sum*' ('I think, therefore I am').

Most modern philosophers restrict the *a priori* to tautologies (sometimes called **analytic** sentences). As the *cogito* is not analytic, they would therefore reject this as a tautology ('existing' is not part of the definition of 'thinking' in the way that having four sides is essential to the definition of a square). But they would often include mathematics, on the grounds that all mathematical calculations are variations on the basic tautological truth that $x = x$. That is the result of all sums: $694 + 6 = 700$ is simply a variation. Those of us who find mathematics difficult may regret that examiners do not accept $x = x$ as the answer to every question.

Some philosophers, such as St Anselm and Descartes, have attempted to prove the existence of God *a priori* – we will see their theories in the chapter on Ontological Arguments.

Many philosophers point out two things about tautologies:

1. Their truth is certain because we make them so by the rules of our language – that is why mathematics is certain. We make the rules by which $2 + 2 = 4$ is true. If someone showed us a triangle and said 'this is square', we would tell him he was wrong – without four sides we would not allow the word 'square' to be used.
2. They tell us no facts, no truths about the world. For example, 'A mermaid is half-woman, half-fish' is certainly true, because that is what we mean by the word 'mermaid', but whether mermaids actually exist as beings in the world is not knowable without sense experience. Tautologies are definitions about the meanings of words.

A posteriori

This refers to those things knowledge of which depends on sense experience. In a descriptive sentence which is not a tautology, there are some things which can be known to be true by looking or using our senses in some other way. No knowledge of the meaning of the words will tell us whether 'my cat is playing with a ball' is true: someone needs to look to test whether it is so.

A problem to notice at once is that any sense experience has limitations. We can only perceive the word with the senses we have – there is nowhere outside ourselves we can go to check whether our perceptions are accurate. If we read books or see films to check what is out there, we still read those books, see those films, with our own eyes. We can never certainly know that the world is as it seems to us to be – we can only know that that is how it appears to us.

To think about this a little more, consider the sentence, 'That chair is blue.' How do we know whether the chair has any kind of existence beyond our imaginations, that outside what is me is this other, not-me object, the chair? I see it as blue. All I really know is that I describe it as blue. I may hear the other object I think of as 'you' also describing the chair as blue. The most I could know is that you use the term 'blue' to describe the chair. I do not know what blue looks like to you. I cannot get inside your mind to share your subjective understanding of what blue feels like or looks like, any more than I can know what something you like and I do not tastes like to you.

There is always a question over *a posteriori* judgements, because they can never be wholly certain. That they are uncertain is unavoidable, but it need not be a reason for despair. After all, there are many things in life like that. We do not withhold friendship because we cannot *prove* that our best friend will never betray us, and there is no reason to despair of all our knowledge because we are aware of its limitations.

There is a significant difference between genuine philosophical doubt and other sorts of doubt. A good test about doubt is to ask whether a particular doubt is reasonable. A lecturer was talking to his students, and said: 'Walls cannot think.'

One of his students replied: 'How do you know they cannot?'

The lecturer responded that there was no evidence that walls could think – they have no brain or nervous system, nor anything we associate with thought, neither was there any evidence that they had ever thought.

'But,' said the student, 'they might . . .'

In theory, perhaps, but ought we to entertain a doubt when there is no good reason for that doubt? And that is what is essential to real philosophical doubt – there must be grounds for it. There are good philosophical reasons for doubting arguments for the existence of God – as there are also for rejecting atheism – and the good philosopher, regardless of personal belief, pays attention to these.

Knowledge and Belief

When can we claim that we *know* something, and not simply that we *believe* it?

Philosophers generally agree on four criteria of when we can claim knowledge:

1. What we believe to be true must in fact be true. I can hardly be said to *know* that Snowdon is the world's highest mountain when it is not.
2. We must really believe that what we believe is true, is true. If someone said: 'I think Paris is the capital of France, but I'm really not sure,' we would not say he had *knowledge*.
3. We must be fully justified in believing what we do – that is, we must have good reasons for our belief. This is a difficult question as there is great debate about what counts as sufficient justification.
4. Our belief must not rest on any false information. I could hardly be said to *know* that Everest is the highest mountain if I said I knew it because it says so in the Bible – the Bible does not mention Everest.

> ## !!! WARNING NOTICE!!!
>
> Not all philosophers accept the part about justification, believing that there are problems in justifying any belief. A key thinker who takes this view is Professor Sir Michael Dummett, who coined the term *anti-realist* for this notion. Much has been written about this debate, much of it being misunderstood, sometimes by people who ought to know better. One would think from some authors that every philosopher is either a realist or an anti-realist. D. Z. Phillips, one of the most significant philosophers of religion in recent years, attacked both realism and anti-realism, pointing out that one could, as he did, reject both views.
>
> Our advice is to ignore this difficult debate and not to discuss the issue. Examiners do not require any knowledge of anti-realism at A level, and it is better to say nothing than to get it wrong.

It is important to pay attention to these claims about knowledge. Especially on religious, as sometimes on political matters, people claim to *know* things that really they do not – people claim to 'know' there is a God, or to 'know' there is none. They may have good reasons for their belief, and certainly be sincere in holding it, but it would be wrong to say they have knowledge.

Logic

This is the branch of Philosophy which concerns itself with the structure of arguments. Its primary concern is not whether a particular argument is true, but rather the structure that, if the elements were true, would yield true conclusions.

This is most easily understood in practice. Aristotle is often considered the father of logic – he was especially interested in the forms of argument which led to true conclusions. Indeed, until the beginning of the twentieth century, all logic was based on the principles which he had set out in the fourth century before Christ.

The Syllogism

Aristotle's logic is sometimes referred to as the Syllogistic, because the *syllogism* is the most basic logical form within the system.

A syllogism has a minimum of three elements: a *major premise*, a *minor premise* and a *conclusion*.

Perhaps the most famous syllogism is the following:

All men are mortal (*Major Premise*)
Socrates is a man (*Minor Premise*)
Therefore: Socrates is mortal (*Conclusion*)

What makes the first line a major premise is that it is an 'all' sentence. The argument would not work if, instead of 'all' we wrote 'some' or even 'most' – Socrates might then be one of those men not mortal. A major premise is always universal (it could, of course be 'none' rather than 'all', as long as the term excludes any exception – remember that it is the exception which disproves the rule).

The minor premise is a particular piece of information – in this case, about Socrates. The important thing to notice is that it is the structure of the argument which makes the conclusion true. The form of the argument is:

All *p* are *q*
r is *p*
Therefore *r* is *q*

We can see quite easily that any argument of this form will give us a true conclusion if the premises are true.

Consider this:

All Martians have two heads
Adolf Hitler was a Martian
Therefore Adolf Hitler had two heads.

We hope to offend no Martians among our readers . . . But we can see that if the two premises were true (we do not believe they are), then the conclusion would necessarily follow.

Notice that we can say that the conclusion that Hitler was two-headed is *logical* – it follows logically from what has gone before in the argument. The term 'logical' does not mean the same as 'true' or even 'sensible' – something is logical when it necessarily follows from certain premises. And an argument which gives true conclusions when the premises are true is called a *valid* argument. Our argument about Hitler is valid, as, if the premises were true, than obviously the argument would be.

This type of argument is also called a *deductive* argument – the conclusion is based on the premises and is deducible from them.

Many philosophers, including David Hume, argue that our knowledge of the outside world is not of this kind. They say that most of our science – apart from mathematics, which is deductive – is based on making general conclusions from many observations. So, for example, we note enormous numbers of instances of the sun rising every morning, and draw the general conclusion: 'The sun rises every morning.' This becomes a principle of geography and astronomy. But, of course, the conclusion is at best only probable – there could still be the exception, when the sun burns itself out. This kind of reasoning, called *inductive*, can only give us probabilities at best.

But induction involves the logical Problem of Induction. The problem is simply explained – the only proof we have that many instances of events give us probable general conclusions is the many instances of events giving us probable general conclusions. The only evidence for induction is induction itself.

Three Basic Logical Principles

Over the centuries, many different logical principles have been developed, many of which are variants on three straightforward notions which you should know:

1. *Identity.*   This is an easy one, as it is assumed in every piece of algebra you have ever studied. It is the basic truth that $x = x$, or that *something is (identical to) itself.* It may seem too obvious to be worth saying as we take it for granted when we do a sum that, in $2 + 2 = 4$, the terms retain their meaning – the second 2 is identical in meaning with the first 2. If it did not, even the most basic mathematics would be impossible.
2. *Non-contradiction.*   There is no mystery about this – it is the assumption that a contradiction is not logically possible. That is, no thing with a quality has the negative of that quality. So, a mermaid cannot be not-woman/not-fish, a square cannot have the quality of circularity, and so on. Philosophically, no sentence can be true and false at the same time.
3. *Excluded Middle.*   This simply says that everything either has a quality or the negative of that quality – it cannot have that both. Either I am a man or I am not – I cannot at the same time and in the same way be both a man and not.

STRETCH AND CHALLENGE

None of the theories we have considered is unproblematic, but there is no need at this stage to be aware of all the issues. Two points, however, might interest you.

Modern Logic

At the end of the nineteenth century there were enormous developments in mathematics. The key point was the realization that mathematics consisted of systems of definitions and rules, such as counting in tens, or two negatives making a positive, or geometry working in three dimensions. If mathematicians changed the systems of rules, then they could devise new systems of mathematics. And so, mathematicians began to develop new geometries and other new mathematical systems.

Many great mathematicians have also been great philosophers. Among these were Gottlob Frege (1848–1925) in Germany, and Bertrand Russell (1872–1970) and his British collaborator, Alfred North Whitehead (1861–1947) in Britain. *Principia Mathematica* (3 volumes, 1910–13), by Russell and

Whitehead, transformed our understanding of mathematics and logic. The simple point was that if new mathematical languages could be created by changing the rules, so too could new systems of logic, using different axioms.

At the same time, a further challenge to traditional views of logic was made by the Polish philosopher, Jan Łukasiewicz (1878–1956), in 1918. Most philosophers had taken the view that significant sentences are either true or false, but there were always puzzle sentences, such as 'The Battle of Salamis will take place tomorrow', or ' "All Cretans are liars," said the Cretan', which had worried the Greeks as clearly they mean something, but are paradoxical – if true, they are false, if false they are true (Think about it!). Łukasiewicz dealt with the problem by saying that there were other values than true and false, opening the way to the development of neuter-valued logics by philosophers such as Czesław Lejewski. Together, the logicians made possible the many logical languages at the heart of the computer revolution.

These points are valuable for certain areas in the Philosophy of Religion – see the Stretch and Challenge box in the chapter on The Ontological Argument.

Induction

Some philosophers have attacked the entire notion of induction. Sir Karl Popper (1902–94) argued that we just do not learn by induction. He says we do not in practice collect vast numbers of instances and *then* draw a conclusion from them. Rather, we notice a feature of the world, form a theory (a *hypothesis*) about it, then *deduce* what would test and disprove the hypothesis. Then we test it. His argument is based on the fact that we are by nature constructors of theories. I see the same person pass my front gate every day at 8.30, see him return at 4.30, and form a theory that he teaches at the school up the road. If I were nosey enough, I could then be able to work out how to test whether my theory was true or not. Popper points out also that high probability does not count in favour of a theory – after all, every day the sun rises, it does not become more probable that it will rise the next day, as we draw closer to the time when the sun burns itself out.

This attack on inductivism is worth bearing in mind as David Hume and Richard Swinburne, both major figures in the Philosophy of Religion, base their arguments very largely on inductive assumptions and probability.

Exercise

Although you will not be asked questions directly on the material in this chapter, the knowledge here will be presupposed in other answers.

This exercise tests your knowledge in part a) and your ability to assess a case in part b). Use the mark allocation as a guide to length – you should spend about half an hour on these questions.

a. **Explain the difference between *a priori* and *a posteriori* knowledge. [25 marks]**

b. **'We can be sure of nothing about the facts of the world.' Discuss. [10 marks]**

Plato and the Doctrine of the Forms 2

Socrates and Plato

Central to any understanding of Plato is his relationship to Socrates (469–399 BC). Socrates, often called the Father of Philosophy, is a fascinating figure. By trade a stonemason, he was a well-known figure in Athens.

It is always helpful to remember that Ancient Greece is often best understood as a culture, even an idea. Greeks separated themselves from non-Greeks, who were literally the barbarians. But what we call Greece was not a single nation-state or Empire, as Rome would be, but a collection of smaller enclaves, often misleadingly called 'city-states'. Some, like Macedonia, extended well beyond a single city, while others, such as Ithaca, did not boast a city. The Greek term for one of these units was *polis*, from which we get the word 'politics'. Each *polis* developed its own system of government, some as kingdoms, like Macedonia, or Ithaca, some with other forms. Sparta, the toughest, had two kings. Athens was unique – it was a democracy, which meant that the people came together to make the great decisions. Of course, the people did not include women, foreigners, slaves or children. But this was a direct democracy, with people meeting together in the *agora* or marketplace, to make the great decisions of state, appointing the generals, deciding on the laws, on war, and so on. This was a direct democracy, unlike our indirect democracy, in which we appoint people to make decisions on our behalf. Socrates was a brave soldier, who, when on duty, was struck – so legend has it – by a vision, which led him to believe himself attended by a personal spirit, a daemon, which would tell him when he was right.

Whatever the truth of the matter, there is no doubt that on his return to Athens, to his wife's legendary annoyance (she at least once tipped a chamber pot on his head), devoted much of his time to going about talking about philosophical questions, especially about what it means to be a good man. He would work by a process of questions, trapping his listeners into confusion, but with the aim of getting to the truth. He would be a guest at dinner parties, leading conversation. As such he became a cult figure among various young men of Athens, including Plato and his brothers.

But politics took a hand. In the Athenian army, a young soldier was made to share a tent with an older one. It was expected that they would become lovers, the rationale being that if you were in love with the soldier standing next to you in line of battle, you would fight all the harder on his behalf. Socrates' young lover was Alcibiades. The latter rose to become a general in the long-running war with Sparta, but turned traitor, going over to the Spartan side. Socrates was known to admire many aspects of Sparta, and was tainted by association.

Socrates was arrested and charged with impiety and corrupting the morals of the youth of Athens. He was put on trial, and determined on his own defence. (In Athens, no lawyers were permitted in court to act to defend the accused. But most accused would go to the Sophists, professionals in constructing arguments, to find persuasive arguments, and then to the Orators, who would teach how to be heard by and to persuade an audience). Socrates determined to defend himself (it is a truism among modern barristers that a man who defends himself has a fool for a client). He was convicted and sentenced to death. He was given every opportunity to escape, but refused, and died by drinking hemlock.

As mentioned, one of the young men around him was Aristicles (427–347 BC), nicknamed Plato, meaning 'broad', from his success as a wrestler. He had originally hoped for a career in politics. Instead, embittered by the actions of the Athenian democracy in killing Socrates, he devoted himself to continuing the work of Socrates. In 387, in the Groves of Akademe, he founded a school, known to us as the Academy, where he would teach for the remainder of his life. Plato had colossal literary skill, and he wrote a series of dialogues, in which Socrates was the main character. We believe that what Plato has Socrates say in the early dialogues is close to what the historical Socrates actually did say. But in the later dialogues, Socrates becomes a mouthpiece for Plato's own views. We can be fairly sure of this, even though Socrates himself wrote nothing (he may have been illiterate), because the Doctrine of the Forms becomes central. It was not mentioned in the early dialogues. If Socrates had made it central, one would have expected it to be mentioned earlier – one would not write twenty books about Einstein before mentioning relativity. The most famous of these later dialogues is *The Republic*.

Plato on the Soul

The key to understanding Plato is to recognize that he was a dualist, believing in two entities, the body and the soul. Plato's view of the soul was that it is a simple sub-stance – it just *is*. As it is a simple substance it cannot be destroyed. Plato thought that to be destroyed meant to be broken to pieces. As a simple substance, the soul cannot disintegrate, as it has no parts into which it could disintegrate (Immanuel Kant pointed out that nevertheless its intensity could dwindle to nothing).

We need to say at once that this is a soul very different from the Christian concep-tion. No Christian could accept that the soul is eternal because that is the kind of thing it is – to say *nothing* can destroy it would diminish the power of God. For the Chris-tian, eternal life is a gift of God, not an inevitability. The other difference from the Christian view is that, for Plato, the eternity of the soul means not merely that the soul will always exist, but that it *has* always existed. Christians believe that the soul begins at conception.

In having this view, Plato has created a problem for himself – in his metaphysics, he has to account not simply for the destiny of the soul, but where it has been.

The Doctrine of the Forms

Plato was deeply influenced by Pythagoras (he of the Theorem), who believed that the ultimate constituent of the universe was number. To the Pythagoreans, numbers were real things, rather as we might think of atoms. Now, it is a feature of any two numbers that they are in ratio to each other. Pythagoreans see the universe as filled with ratios – it is essentially harmonious, with everything in relation to everything else.

Plato believed that there exist two kinds of beings: spiritual essences (such as souls) and material beings (such as gerbils, tables, daffodils, bodies and so on). Each has its proper realm – the realm of reality and the realm of appearances.

If we look at this material realm, where we live, everything changes and dies, but souls, being simple, are eternal and unchanging. So, for Plato, parallel with this world, there exists an unchanging and permanent realm which is the realm of souls. Because this does not decay, it is true reality. Plato was influenced – how much is a matter of argument – by the thought of the philosopher Heraclitus, who flourished around

500 BC. He was famous for his notion that we cannot step into the same river twice, but his importance here is that he believed in an underlying stability and harmony in this world of change. Plato sought to articulate this vision, and his realm of the forms gives the certainty and fixity so obviously absent from this earthly life.

Think for the moment of the chair on which you may be sitting. How do you know that it is a chair? The answer you might give is that you have seen chairs before, and it is like them, which is how you recognized it as a chair when you met it for the first time. That is, incidentally, the answer Aristotle (next chapter – do not be too impatient!) might have given. But it is not Plato's answer. Remember that the realm of reality parallels this one.

For Plato, you know that this is a chair because you have a more or less clear memory of the Ideal Form of the chair. Remember that we are, for Plato, a mixture of everlasting soul and temporary body. This means that the soul originally belonged in the realm of pure spirit – the realm of reality or the Realm of the Forms. For reasons which are not altogether clear, at some point we entered into bodies and were born. This was deeply traumatic – so traumatic that we cannot even remember being born. The process drove out clear recollection of our past life, but, deep down, our souls know they do not belong in this world of temporary things which decay, this Realm of Appearances.

But the Realm of the Forms not merely has human souls, it has other types of soul – the Ideal Forms. Among those is the one perfect Form of the chair – everlasting, without decay. The chairs we make are copies of that Form – the better a chair, the closer it is to the Form, but, of course, even the best material chairs fall apart eventually. One can understand how this idea might be derived. Have you ever noticed how, when we make something, we begin with an idea, but that what we actually make is never as good as our original mental picture of it? Making begins with the idea – for Plato, therefore, we are copying the more or less clear *recollection* of the Form of the chair.

This idea has certain consequences. No one invents anything – the first human maker of the first vacuum cleaner is simply the first person clearly to remember the original Form. Plato believed also that education did not mean putting things into a child's mind, but drawing out what was already present there. And the good chair-maker is simply one who has thought harder about the idea of the chair.

Behind this is his sense of ratio and harmony. Remember that this world parallels the Realm of the Forms, and is in a kind of ratio to it. So, if something is the case in this world, it must be even more true in the Realm of the Forms. In this world, all life depends on warmth and light from the sun. We would not be able to see the objects of this world without light from the sun. In the same way, our mental powers need something in the spiritual realm to enable us to understand the truth in the Forms. So, just as we have the sun supreme over appearances, there must be a supreme Form, the

Form of the Good, which gives life to the other Forms and understanding to the mind to enable us to have any knowledge of them. (Plato restricts the term 'knowledge' to knowledge of the forms. As our perceptions of this world are uncertain, and the things in it are shifting, Plato calls our awareness of these *doxa*, or opinion/belief.) So the highest knowledge is knowledge of the Form of the Good. No knowledge can be certain but that. He thought further that the only people who look beyond beautiful – and imperfect – things in this world and ask 'What is good in itself?' are philosophers. From this, in the *Republic*, he argued that only philosophers were truly fit to rule. (He shared a common Greek view that if one knows what is right one is bound to do it – wrongdoing is always the result of ignorance. It was partly a problem of language – Greek did not have a word for *will* and consequently lacked explanations such as weakness of will for doing bad things.)

The Form of the Good presents particular problems. It is not to be thought of as the Creator – it is not a Christian God by another name. It is not quite clear exactly what it is. Things that we call good somehow participate in the Form of the Good – their goodness, imperfect though it is, is a reflection of the one true Good. Plato suggests that in this world, the sun gives both life to being, as without light we and the plants and animals would not grow and flourish, and provides light by which these things can be seen. In the same way, the Form of the Good is the source of the goodness in everything else, including the forms, and gives understanding to the mind in the same way that the sun gives sight to the eyes. But the other forms are not identical with the Form of the Good, any more than the plants or animals are identical with the sun.

In the *Republic*, Plato has Socrates promise his listeners the clear account of the Form of the Good that he owes them, then give by his own admission simply images of the good, by use of similes. By doing so, he opens the debate, which remains unsettled, of what precisely he did mean.

The Simile of the Cave

In the *Republic*, Plato illustrates his theory by three similes – of the Sun, the Divided Line and, most famously, the Cave.

Think of an underground cave. In it, prisoners are chained with their backs to a wall. They have been there all their lives. Behind the wall is a road, and behind that, higher up, is a fire. People walk along the road, carrying various models of things – animals, and other things, on poles. The fire projects shadows of these things onto the wall in front of the prisoners. The prisoners, who can only look directly in front of them, know no other reality than the shadows, around which they create their own reality. They play games of guessing which shadow will come next.

One of the prisoners is suddenly released. He turns around and discovers the fire and the rest of the things behind the prisoners. At first, the fire is too bright to look at, but then he becomes used to the light and sees more clearly.

The cave represents the Realm of Appearances – this world in which we live. The shadows on the wall represent images, shadows, paintings and illusions of all kinds. The fire represents the sun which gives light to this world. The objects carried on poles, and the other things in the cave, represent the things we see around us in this world.

Then the prisoner is forcibly dragged upwards out of the cave into the true sunlight. At first he will be utterly dazzled, and be able to look only at shadows. By this, Plato is representing mathematical knowledge. (Mathematicians obviously deal with abstract thought, like philosophers, but they begin from assumptions, such as numbers and geometrical shapes, and then reason what *follows* from them. Philosophers, on the other hand, ask what triangles and numbers are in themselves – they look directly *to* the Forms.)

Next the released prisoner is able to look at the objects of the upper world. These obviously represent the Forms themselves – these are the real animals and vases of which those carried by men in the cave were only copies. The very last thing the prisoner can look at is the sun, which of course represents the Form of the Good.

Plato goes on to describe what happens when the prisoner returns to the cave. His fellow prisoners do not believe the tales he tells them of the upper world, and discover that his eyes have become unaccustomed to the gloom – he is worse at the games than he was before. They may even kill him. Here, Plato is clearly thinking of the death of Socrates by people unable to see the great truths he could see. Those who killed him were not intrinsically wicked, but were ignorant, hence their foolish act.

This simile works at many levels, illustrating both the theory of the forms and his reasons for thinking that philosophers were the most fitted for rule, knowing reality as it is. It also graphically demonstrates the nature of philosophical enlightenment.

Criticisms of Plato

The doctrine of the Forms has been heavily criticized. Plato's pupil, Aristotle, famously rejected the notion, even while a pupil of the Academy. He lists a whole series of objections to the Forms and, in particular, the Form of the Good, in *Nicomachean Ethics*, Book I, Chapter vi. You might usefully look at the three or four pages of this chapter to see which arguments appeal especially to you.

Some of Aristotle's objections are:

- Good comes in so many varieties that there cannot be a single Form of it. The goodness of a person is very different from being a good shovel, a good meal, a good painting, a good horse, or whatever. Someone who is a good person may be a very bad shovel, and a good rider may be a bad person.
- Something does not have to be eternal to have a pure quality. Something white does not become more white by being eternal as far as its whiteness is concerned – eternity and whiteness are different qualities.
- The Forms have no practical use. If they were so essential to understanding, then why have people not paid attention to them? But we do not work that way. A doctor does not think of the ideal form of health – even if there were such a thing – when she treats a patient. What is healthy for a ninety-year-old woman is very different from what is healthy for an eighteen-year-old man. The doctor does not ask what is healthy in itself, but what is healthy for this patient.
- There are incoherencies within the general theory of the Forms. Some things have no form, where problems become too great – there is no Form of Number – only Forms of oneness, twoness and so on. (This, Aristotle might have added, creates interesting problems – an infinity of numbers suggests an infinity of Forms, creating its own problems.) This also assumes that numbers are real things.

The Influence of Plato

The influence of Plato was very great. Not merely did the Dialogues survive, but the Academy thrived for hundred of years. Especially important was the sharp division between body and soul, the spiritual and the material. This approach would dominate Greek thought, contrasting the temporary nature of this world with the permanence of our heavenly home, a place purely spiritual and permanent.

Remember that the New Testament was written in Greek. Jesus was a Jew who almost certainly did not read Greek (he probably spoke some as Nazareth was a major trading post for Greek merchants, and the Roman soldiers in Palestine used Greek rather than Latin). But the writers were fluent in Greek and Greek patterns of thought. So too were most of the early Fathers of the Church. It was perhaps natural that Christian ideas would be cast in Platonic terms. Jesus himself does not make the sharp distinction between body and soul that would become common in many strands of Christianity – he saves men and women, not simply their souls. Christianity has repeatedly struggled with heresies – including Gnosticism, Catharism (Albigensianism), Manichaeanism, the Bogomils and others – which tended to deny the body and material things. When St Paul went to Athens, many of the Greeks struggled above all with the materialism of Christianity, with its insistence on bodily resurrection. And this is why, in the Creeds, it was necessary (but to many scandalous) to insist on God as creator of *all* things, visible and invisible, spiritual *and* material. It is interesting to reflect on how many religious believers can still struggle with questions of the material. They can easily think of Christ as God, but struggle with the thought of him as someone who needed to cut his toenails, relieve himself, and do all those things which are part of bodily life.

STRETCH AND CHALLENGE

An interesting objection to Plato's theories can be developed on lines suggested by, among others, the Polish logician and philosopher Tadeusz Kotarbiński (1886–1981).

This approach suggests that Plato is guilty of a mistake about language – the mistake of *reification*. If we think about this, we recognize that because we have a word for something, we assume that there is a thing to which that name belongs. The reason for the confusion is simple – in our grammar there are words which we call *nouns*, that is, names, and we assume that if we have a name, there exists something corresponding to that name. But there are some words which function grammatically as nouns, but which are not themselves names. For example, in the sentence, 'There is nothing there', *nothing* is a noun, but it does not name a thing – there is no something which is nothing – it would be a contradiction in terms. This is true of other terms. There is no such thing as justice – people are just, judges may be just, and so on, but, these philosophers would argue, there is no justice over and above people who are just, no love which exists outside those beings which are loving and so on. There is no relationship between two people other than that they are related. We could reconstruct the sentence, 'There is a relationship between Jules and Jim', removing the noun 'relationship' and saying, instead, 'Jules and Jim are related'. Philosophers like Kotarbiński argue that questions such as 'What is love?' make no sense, though many questions may be asked about what it means to be loving or to be loved. (The logical term for an apparent noun – a word that functions grammatically as a noun without naming real beings – is an *onomatoid*.)

If these theories are right, perhaps Plato's problem was that he had words such as 'Good', 'Justice', 'Beauty' and so on, could find no corresponding entities in this world, and constructed another world in which they might have being.

It is perhaps also worth noting Karl Popper's argument that Plato sought permanence as a refuge from this uncertain and shifting world – many seek a permanence because they find uncertainty difficult to cope with. It may be that an uncertain world is all there is.

Exercise and Examination Advice

Make a list of the following terms in your notes and make sure you research them until you have a clear understanding of what each means:

Analogy

Prisoners

The Instructor

Cave

Shadows

The Outside World

The Sun

Journey

Forms

Concepts

Phenomena

Ideals

The Form of the Good

As we have indicated elsewhere, preparing specific essays is a two-edged sword when it comes to preparing for examinations; if you are lucky enough to have that question turn up, you can do very well. If it does not then you may find yourself trying to make your answer fit into the question, a process my daughter calls 'twisting the question'. This is rarely a good idea.

It is much better to make sure, in this case, that you understand all the terms Plato uses and that you are able to apply them to any question the examiner sets. One of the things we are examining is your ability to **select** the correct material from your revision and use it to construct a coherent and critical answer to the specific question set the year you are sitting the exam.

So you could be asked, for example, to demonstrate your understanding of the role of the inner world of the cave in Socrates' discussion. While this does mean demonstrating a general understanding of the analogy of the cave, it is not really asking you to just write out the bits you remember. Clearly the context of the prisoners is very important and you will show that you understand the constrictions under which they live; however, the focus of this particular answer has to be on the role of the shadows to the prisoners and what happens when one particular prisoner faces the light coming from the fire, noting that this is before the prisoner has even left the cave. Many students think that the pain starts after he leaves the cave, because they have not studied the text carefully enough.

In the B section you will be asked to demonstrate evaluative skills. Here you should not be demonstrating knowledge and understanding; you should already have done that. This time you should be using the knowledge and understanding to write a critique of what Plato is trying to say, again focusing on whichever aspect of these teachings the question is examining. You may for example be asked to evaluate the extent to which Plato was criticizing the people of Athens, who had, after all, in his eyes, unfairly executed his teacher, Socrates. Alternatively, if you had been asked to explain the Forms in part A then you could be asked to write some sort of evaluation of the extent to which Plato's view of the world is reasonable or indeed has any basis whatsoever in reality.

It is important to note that none of the above constitutes a full answer to questions. They are approaches which could be applied to any question the examiner may ask. All you need to do is make sure you understand the areas thoroughly and to think through your own views about what Plato is saying.

You could now, perhaps, try answering the following question yourself:

a. **Describe the meaning of the shadows in the analogy of the cave. [25]**

b. **'Plato is wrong to think the shadows are unreal.' Discuss. [10]**

Aristotle 3

Introduction

The great Italian poet, Dante, called Aristotle the 'Master of those who know' – his significance is immense, not least on the Philosophy of Religion. In this chapter, it is not possible to develop the full range of his incredibly wide-ranging thought, but we shall concentrate on his method and his significance for our subject.

Aristotle (384–322 BC) was the greatest of Plato's pupils – he was a student from 367 until Plato's death in 347, and, although he would profoundly disagree with Plato, especially as we have seen, over the Forms, he never lost his respect and affection for his master. He is reputed to have said: 'Plato is dear to us, but truth is more dear', and he writes often of Plato as a friend.

Three biographical facts are crucial to understanding Aristotle:

1. He was born 15 years after the death of Socrates, and so never felt the death in the same way as the direct experience it was to Plato, just as to a child born in 2012 the death of Diana, Princess of Wales will always be history, however much it might have meant to the parents. Aristotle's approach to thought was not

coloured by the bitterness of Plato over the execution. Neither did he feel the same need to justify Socrates' accepting his death.

2. He was not an Athenian. Aristotle was born in Stagira, in the kingdom of Macedonia. In Athens, he was never part of the citizenry, so he viewed the democracy as an outsider. He did not share a number of Athenian attitudes, for example strongly disagreeing with the homosexuality taken for granted in Athens. As well as his rejection of the Forms, his foreignness may also have been an explanation for his being passed over as principal of the Academy after Plato's death.

3. His father was a doctor, court physician to Amyntas, King of Macedonia, and thereafter to King Philip the Great. Aristotle retained a lifelong interest in medicine, and many of his examples refer to doctors and health. Thinking about medicine is immensely helpful to understanding his rejection of the Forms and his approach to understanding both humans and knowledge in general.

Aristotle on Knowledge

Imagine yourself as a doctor, confronted by a patient covered in spots. Your task is to treat him. Suppose you followed a Platonic view, that knowing the ideal form of health would somehow give you all the practical knowledge needed to treat your patient, just as Plato thought knowing the Form of the Good would somehow give you the practical skills to rule a state. It is difficult to know precisely how you would get this practical skill.

Aristotle's approach is quite different. If you want to know about spots, the way to do so is to look at spots. The only way you will know the difference between the spots of measles and those of smallpox, chickenpox, acne or any other type of spot is through experience of spots. At the heart of Aristotle's approach is the belief that knowledge rests on careful observation. If you want to learn how to be a good person, you will not learn it through a knowledge of good in the abstract, but by observing the people we call good and seeing what it is that leads us to describe them in that way. Aristotle's work is characterized by careful observation, reflection on and categorization of phenomena. His preferred method was *per genus et per differentia*, that is, by type and by difference, so, if I come across a cat, I learn about it by seeing what sort of thing it is – a feline – but then look to see how it differs from other things of that kind, such as lions, tigers and lynxes, so that I can get closer to things in themselves. Aristotle's own greatest scientific discovery, that the earth is round, was the result of his observations of an eclipse of the moon.

Unlike Plato, who treated all knowledge as intellectual, Aristotle argued that we learn in many different ways. Knowing about the geometrical qualities of squares is an intellectual matter, but knowing how to play the harp is not like that. Playing an instrument, making furniture, and indeed, running a state or being a good person, are skills, learned by practice and developing good habits. Many people have great skills, know how to do things, without much theoretical knowledge. If my car breaks down, I prefer the attention of the skilled mechanic to the greatest theorist of mechanical engineering.

Aristotle also disagreed with Plato's quest for absolute precision and certainty. He argued that we can only have as much precision as the subject matter will bear, and that it is the mark of an untrained mind to expect more than this. He says that it would be as unreasonable to accept precision from a teacher of rhetoric as to accept mere plausibility from a mathematician.

Aristotle on Cause – The Theory of the Four Causes

Any understanding of Aristotle depends on understanding of his scientific assumptions. This is why examiners insist on knowledge of his theory of Causation. Without it, many points in his thought, not only in metaphysics but also in Politics and Ethics, become difficult to follow.

As a careful observer of the world, Aristotle believed in the notions of cause and effect. He developed the concept at length in the *Physics*, but the idea is central to all his work. He identified four types of cause that make something what it is:

1. *Material Cause.* This is what something is made from – the material cause of this chair is the plastic and wood and metal from which it is made. Without them, this chair would not exist. Think of this in terms of *stuff* in a general sense. Without its material, nothing would exist.
2. *Formal Cause.* This chair is what it is because it is *in the form of* a chair – that is the shape which the wood, metal etc. have. If it were not that shape, it would not be this chair. Notice that for Aristotle, the form is *in* the chair and each chair has its own form. The transcendence of Plato's single Form is here made immanent and grounded. The material is chair-shaped.
3. *Efficient Cause.* This is what brings the chair about: in this case, the chairmaker. Had there not been an efficient cause, the chair would not exist – something causes it to be, just as certain biological events bring about the daffodil. This efficient cause might be an agent or a natural phenomenon – the cliff is eroded because of the actions of wind and wave on it.
4. *Final Cause.* This is the purpose for which a thing exists, that is, what it is for. The chair exists for the purpose of providing somewhere comfortable to sit, a house to provide shelter, and so on. Aristotle believed that all nature has a

purpose. After all, he argued, each part of the body has a purpose – I have a stomach, heart, lungs, etc., for a purpose, and even my eyebrows keep sweat out of my eyes, and my feet stop my ankles wearing down. In *Nicomachean Ethics*, Aristotle argues that it would be unreasonable to think each part of the person has a purpose, but that the person as a whole does not. This purposiveness of things is incredibly important to Aristotle. When I make a meal, I make it to eat. We do not, he assumes, do things for no reason at all. Neither does nature. Whether this is true, whether things always have a function, is very open to doubt, as we shall see.

Aristotle on God and the Soul

For Aristotle, the soul is the formal cause of the person, but it is not the eternal thing that it was for Plato. The soul is the animating principle of the person – when it dies, the body dies also. He speculated that perhaps reason goes on after our death, though not personal existence, but, unlike Plato, Aristotle teaches no theory of eternal life.

Aristotle believed in a God, but one very unlike the Christian or Islamic belief. For Aristotle, God is perfect and everlasting. Being perfect, he is interested only in perfect things. And the only thing worthy of his contemplation is perfect being – himself. He spends eternity simply contemplating his own wonderful being, uninterested in anything else.

For Aristotle the world is eternal like God – it has always existed. The question of how it was caused does not arise. God's relationship to the earth is as Final Cause – not cause in any modern scientific sense of the term, but as purpose or goal. The best part of the person is the most God-like part of us, the intellect, and the best human activity is the same as that of God – pure contemplation.

Perhaps Aristotle's most distinctive contribution to the theories for the existence of God is his notion of God as **Prime Mover**. St Thomas Aquinas would use this notion as the first of his Five Ways – it is an important element in his Cosmological Argument.

By motion, Aristotle meant more than simply the movement of an object from here to there, as when a football is kicked, or a stone thrown through my greenhouse window. For Aristotle, motion means also change, as for example, when a piece of coal becomes hot – it moves from potential (it is capable of being hot) to actuality (it has become the hot thing it was capable of becoming). The cause of change must be external to the thing itself – something outside heats the coal. Aristotle argues that something capable of being heated, such as coal, or moved, such as a football, has to be heated or moved by something itself actually hot (like fire) or moving (like a footballer's boot). Therefore, argues Aristotle, the beginning of the chain which leads to the change must itself be unchanging – it must be actual and not potential. In short, there must be an unmoved mover, the Prime Mover, itself unmoved by something else. For Aquinas, this of course would be the God of Christian theism.

Objections to Aristotle

The most obvious area of objection to Aristotle's views is his assumption that nature is purposive – is *teleological* (from the Greek *telos*, which means goal or target). Is this true?

Consider the human body. It is not immediately clear that *every* part of the body has a purpose. It has recently been argued that the appendix serves a purpose in trapping harmful bacteria in the gut, but what is the purpose of those bacteria? Even if it were true that each part of the human body serves a purpose, does it follow that the person as a whole has a purpose? Aristotle may be guilty of the *error of composition*, which is the mistake of assuming that because something is true of all the parts, the same must be true of the whole. (We shall see this question again in a later chapter.)

Has the mosquito a purpose except being a mosquito? It is difficult to see what good it does. Surely having a purpose is a mental process. People have purposes, but inanimate things do not. I may build a wall for a purpose, even a cathedral, but it is my purpose for which I build it. The wall or cathedral has no sense of purpose – and probably the mosquito has none. To say the wall has a purpose is not strictly true – the builder had a purpose for it, but the purpose is external to the wall itself.

Existentialism reacted against Aristotelianism by arguing that things just are – they exist. Only people have purposes, and those they choose for themselves – they are not born with them. Even if we reject other aspects of Existentialism, it contains fundamental criticisms of Aristotle's approach.

Against the Prime Mover, it is perfectly possible to argue that Aristotle, and, subsequently, Aquinas, are appealing to the fact that we cannot *imagine* an endless chain of movements – surely, we say, it must have a beginning. But, if we think about it, it does not mean, because we cannot imagine an endless chain, that it is impossible. There are many things we cannot imagine, such as being unconscious, or nothing, or, if death is the end of all thought, being dead. But we understand the idea of being unconscious or of nothing, just as we understand the meaning of eternity. That we cannot imagine something tells us something about the limits of our imaginations, but nothing at all about whether something is actually impossible. Logically, something is only impossible if it involves terms which are actually contradictory, such as a 'square circle'. This point about what we can conceive and what we can imagine will become crucial when we consider objections to cosmological arguments.

Aristotle's Legacy

In many ways, Aristotle's work would suffer compared with that of Plato. After his failure to become head of the Academy, he spent some years abroad, including as tutor to Alexander, son of Philip. After Philip's murder, Aristotle wandered before, in the last decade of his life, creating his own school, the Lyceum, in a gymnasium complex to the east of Athens. Although this would survive his death, his own teaching would be neglected, while the Academy always devoted itself to Plato's ideas.

Aristotle's own books disappeared. Those that have come down to us, intended for publication, are marginal – a fragment of the *Constitution of Athens* and a list of winners of the Pythian games. What survived was rather notes for Aristotle's various courses in the Lyceum, perhaps his own teaching notes supplemented by his students. The major works read like notes rather than polished prose. But they are very detailed.

These works themselves were largely lost to Western Europe. They went east, where they would be fundamental to Arabic thought and to the growth of science. By the year 1000 none of Aristotle's work was available in the West in anything approaching its original form.

What was known, second-hand, were details of Aristotle's logical works. The Greek Neoplatonist Porphyry (c.232–c.304) had written an introduction to Aristotle's *Categories*, known as the *Isagogue*.

Most significant had been the work of the Roman, Boethius (c.480–524) who translated Aristotle's logical works (known as the *Organon*, and comprising *Categories, On Interpretaion, Prior Analytics, Topics, Sophistical Refutations* and *Posterior Analytics* – Boethius' translation of the last is now lost). Boethius also translated the *Isagogue*, writing commentaries on that and the *Categories* as well as a lost commentary on *Topics*. He wrote further logical works which develop aspects of Aristotle. The significance of Boethius is difficult to overestimate. To the medievals, he was a revered figure, rivalled only by St Augustine, and his work influenced both St Anselm and St Thomas Aquinas, as we shall see. His work on divine knowledge and the timelessness of God were crucial to theology, but his best-known work was *The Consolation of Philosophy*, written while he was awaiting execution (by having his head slowly crushed). This would be one of the most read works of the Middle Ages, translated into Anglo-Saxon by order of King Alfred and into more modern English by Geoffrey Chaucer in the fourteenth century (even Chaucer's chickens in the *Canterbury Tales* quote Boethius).

Aristotle's works would eventually come into Western Europe during the twelfth and thirteenth centuries, as a consequence of texts brought back during the Crusades, but more particularly through the reconquest of Spain. Greek scholars began to teach throughout Europe, and careful translation of the range of texts, beyond the purely logical, was undertaken at the University of Toledo and elsewhere, including Oxford. Perhaps the finest translator was William of Moerbecke, who provided St Thomas Aquinas with his texts.

Exercises

Firstly make sure you make your own list, with definitions, of the following words:

Cause

Material cause

Efficient cause

Formal cause

Final cause

Prime Mover

You will see that there is less information to learn in this chapter. Once you have studied the context of Aristotle's life and work, there are only two real areas of learning to be covered: what he meant by Cause and the Prime Mover. You will be looking at the Prime Mover in more detail in the next chapter where it is contrasted with the Jewish idea of a Creator.

So, for now, it would be worth focusing your attention towards his ideas about Cause. You may, for example, want to begin by exploring the difference between Plato's ideas of what is real with the completely different way of looking at the universe contained in Aristotle's metaphysics. Any question on this area is likely to ask for some account of the different causes in general as well as asking you to focus on one particular cause.

Try the following:

a. **Explain the four causes in Aristotle. [25]**

b. **'Aristotle's idea about Cause does not help us understand the universe'. Discuss. [10]**

God as the Good Creator

Introduction

In the beginning was the big bang. As the world sprang forth from the fuzzy singularity of its origin, first the special order formed, as quantum fluctuations ceased seriously to perturb gravity. Then space boiled, in the rapid expansion of the inflationary era, blowing the universe apart with incredible rapidity in much less than 10^{-30} seconds that it lasted. The perfect symmetry of the original scheme of things was successively broken as the cooling brought about by expansion crystallized out the forces of nature as we know them today. [1]

Above is a scientific, and in its own way poetic, description of the generally accepted understanding of the beginnings of our universe. As an attempt to describe this event it is not immediately interested in *how* it came about and we will be looking at this concept in more detail later in the book. For now it is important to see this as a modern way of understanding our place in the vast cosmos within which we live. As you will have seen from the previous two chapters, the Greeks had a different but in a sense equally logical and harsh view of the cosmos.

If you are to understand the Jewish concept of creation, then you need to start by understanding their unquestioned assumption that the cosmos is not a cold scientific place in which we struggle to survive, but rather the result of an act of love brought about and sustained by a God who is omnipotent, omnipresent and omniscient.

It is important that you understand this right from the beginning as western Christian philosophy has really been a development of this Jewish understanding within a logical Greek framework; and as you will see later the modern scientific view cannot only fit comfortably into this framework as it developed and was reinterpreted by succeeding generations but may be an integral part of the grand unification theory which scientists are searching so hard to discover.

The Concepts

So before you explore in more detail what the many writers of the book of Genesis mean when they describe God as creator, it is important to understand these concepts.

Firstly omnipotence; literally it means 'all powerful'. Within this lies the idea that nothing logically possible is beyond the power of God. This power is complete and universal. Clearly this does not mean that God can make square circles but that he is responsible for the way the universe works and could if he wanted bend the laws of nature to his will. St Thomas Aquinas would argue that it is no limitation on the power of God not to be able to do the logically impossible. The concept of a square circle is literally meaningless – it is nonsense, just empty words, so there is nothing here for God to do. It is not only to understand the idea of creator that this concept is important, but you will come back to it time and time again. It is crucial, for example, to the framing of the problem of evil, as if God is not omnipotent there is no problem of evil.

Omnipresent is very easy to understand on the surface, simply meaning that God is everywhere and by implication in every moment. What exactly 'every moment' means can become very difficult to grasp, depending which of the many philosophical positions writers are expounding. For the moment, though, it will be best to simply consider this concept in terms of God being everywhere. The joys of time and eternity are best left to the A2 course.

Finally, omniscience: this is the idea that God is all-knowing. There is nothing that happens in the universe physically, mentally or spiritually that God does not know. Again this can be a bit of two-edged sword when it comes to our understanding of God; from the perspective of a loving God it is arguable that an interest and care for everything in the universe is very important. This is not unlike the idea expressed in the Christian gospels which describe God as caring for every sparrow and so much more for humanity. However, if you accept that God knows everything and that he loves us, then why would he allow so many dreadful things to happen throughout the world? There are also questions about the nature of that knowledge. Some argue that

God knows the truth of every true proposition, but there are important questions about how God's eternal knowledge might relate to the world of time in which we find ourselves. Again the details of this will be explored in later chapters but it is important that you grasp the basic meaning here before exploring the implications.

God as Craftsman

Examination board specifications no longer require specific texts to be studied for this part of the course; however, it is clear that a good place to explore this particular concept would be by reading the first three chapters of the book of Genesis. This book is not concerned with fixing a date for creation or describing a detailed scientific account of how God brought it all about. Rather you will find an account of the way God is intimately involved in the making of all the living and non-living things of which the universe consists. In the Revised Standard Version of the Bible, we read in Genesis 1.2:

> The earth was without form and void, and darkness was upon the face of the deep; and the Spirit of God was moving over the face of the waters.

'Spirit of God' is sometimes translated as 'breath of God' and moving as 'brooding'. These versions give the idea not only of God breathing life itself into our world but of a parent 'brooding' over that life. These are images of a God who has intimate and loving involvement in his creation. It is also worth noting that for the Jews, the earth was without form and void. It is as if they thought of existing materials shaped by God. They do not seem to have had a concept at this point of *creatio ex nihilo*, which we will explore below.

Looking beyond the ideas expressed in the early chapters of Genesis, you will find that the idea of God as a craftsman permeates the Old Testament. Many of you will be familiar with the concept of God as a potter.[2] Jeremiah says, in the House of the Potter:

> . . . the word of God came to me as follows, 'House of Israel, can I not do to you what this potter does? Yahweh demands. Yes like clay in the hands of a potter's hands, so you are in mine . . .'

Then he is also seen as a builder in Isaiah,[3] where the prophet says:

> And yet, Yahweh, you are our Father; we the clay and you the potter, all of us the work of your hands.

This image of a craftsman contains within it some challenging notes; being crafted is not always a painless process as you can read in the prophet Malachi,[4] where he says:

He will take his seat as refiner and purifier; he will purify the sons of Levi and refine them like gold and silver, so that they can make the offering to Yahweh with uprightness.

As you will see from these quotations, from the beginning to the end of the Old Testament, this intimate connection between God and his people is integral to the Jewish way of understanding the universe and in a predominately Judaeo-Christian west, fundamental to the development of philosophy. In your examinations you will be expected to be able to compare this view with that of the Greeks you have already studied.

God as Good

This section of the course raises a very interesting question which you will often see expressed as the Euthyphro Dilemma. You will need to consider whether, in a Biblical context, God commands things because they are good or whether things are good because God commands them. The issue is quite significant. Those who follow what is called Divine Command Theory hold that things are right just because God commands them. But think about this for a moment. Suppose God said: 'I command you to rape and pillage and murder.' If Divine Command Theory is correct, these would be right and good actions in themselves. But most believers would say: 'God would not do that', assuming that God would not command them to do bad things. But that would assume there was something in themselves bad about these actions. However, if the wrongness comes from somewhere other than God, does this suggest a limit on God? On the other hand, if whatever God says is right, just because God says it, and for no other reason, would it make any sense to call God good?

While these questions extend through various philosophical writers, for this section of the AS course, you only need to concentrate on where these concepts fit into the Jewish idea of God. This is important as, again, you will see that many assumptions which believers still make are rooted in these Old Testament ideas about God.

It is clear that the Jewish writers had no question in their minds that God was not only good but that all of their own goodness and ethical behaviour flowed from God, and not only that, this was also a God who was morally perfect.

It is in this context that you will see why God can also be seen as both Lawgiver and Judge. Clearly the Decalogue in Exodus 20 would be a good place to begin exploring these ideas, though you are free to use any Jewish teachings in your studies. Recall from Scripture, however, that the Ten Commandments were to remind the Israelites of what they should have known already – after all, Genesis shows many sins, such as the murder of Cain by Abel, happening before the Commandments were revealed to Moses. The Bible does not show killing as wrong just because God tells us not to kill.

Remember that examiners are looking for relevant answers to their questions; they are not limited by a mark scheme. One Old Testament belief which differs significantly from Christian ideas about sin is that you could break laws and be in need of punishment even if you did not know the law existed. This may seem simple enough in terms of ten commandments but you should keep in mind that the Noahide Covenant has 613 commandments. This presents a very different idea of a just lawgiver from a God who would forgive the prodigal son.

In terms of searching for teachings about God's goodness, you need look no further than the first chapter of the first book of the Old Testament; as you already know, God saw that everything he made was good. You do not have to search far to find a significant number of texts which develop this belief; for example the Song of Songs, many of the Psalms or the interesting debate in the Book of Job. The important thing is that when you are finished you have a clear idea of the meaning of these important Jewish beliefs.

Creatio ex nihilo

This phrase '*creatio ex nihilo*' points to the belief among many theists that God created the universe 'out of nothing'. This would mean that before the act of creation there was nothing, no material from which to form a universe. As you will have noted above, this is not the view found in Genesis, though some would argue that it is implied. Reinforcing the idea that this concept is not Jewish is the belief that it came about as a reaction to a form of Gnosticism which saw all matter and material as evil. There was a great deal of philosophical debate around these ideas during the second and third centuries. A clearer statement was put forward by Augustine of Hippo in the late fourth century, where he argued that since God alone is Being, he was able to will to exist what had not existed formerly. In the *Confessions*, Augustine says:

> You did not work as a human craftsman does, making one thing out of something else as his mind directs . . . Your Word alone created . . .[5]

Some would argue that this did not become the formal teaching of the Christian Church until the fourth of the Lateran Councils which took place in 1215. This council stated:

> We firmly believe and openly confess that there is only one true God, eternal and immense, omnipotent, unchangeable, incomprehensible, and ineffable, . . . Creator of all things invisible and visible, spiritual and corporeal, who from the beginning of time and by His omnipotent power **made from nothing** creatures both spiritual and corporeal, angelic, namely, and mundane, and then human, as it were, common, composed of spirit and body.[6]

By the thirteenth century you will find a firm belief among people who are believers which is supported by the canons of this council. This is where you need to be very careful to use sources when you are putting a philosophical argument together. By now you will realize that some writers will see implications in early Jewish texts which lead them to argue for a very early belief in creation *ex nihilo*. Others see it as a Christian interpretation which has nothing to do with their Jewish roots. In examinations you can argue either or both, provided that you justify your opinion.

One final thought, before leaving this teaching. If God created everything out of nothing, then we are left with the question as to whether or not God is responsible for evil in the world. You will look at this in much more detail in later chapters; however, in the present context it will be worth your time to also consider the view of the members of the fourth Lateran Council, where they said:

> The devil and the other demons were indeed created by God good by nature but they became bad through themselves; man, however, sinned at the suggestion of the devil.

Yahweh Compared with Aristotle's Prime Mover

One of the things you may be asked to do in an examination is demonstrate a deep enough understanding of the work you did on Aristotle's Prime Mover to be able to compare this with the Jewish concept of God.

As you have seen, Aristotle did believe in a God, but not at all like the one you have been exploring in this chapter. One of the things which you will study during this course is the different ideas about exactly what the word *eternity* might mean. As you have seen, for Aristotle eternity is connected to perpetual time; so time as such stretches backwards into a past infinity and forwards into a future infinity. It is in this sense that God is eternal or everlasting. Aristotle believed, as you saw earlier, that God is perfect and eternally contemplates his own perfection, uninterested in anything else.

It is from this perspective that Aristotle saw God as the Final Cause, distant and uninvolved with the world. Human beings are called to contemplation and it is in this act that we find God within ourselves. The final part of the Aristotelian idea of God which you need to remember is the concept of God as *Prime Mover*. From whichever angle you approach these Greek concepts of God, it is clear that they present a much more distant and in a sense a more deist idea of God. The Prime Mover is not a being who could be seen as in any sense caring for humanity. However, you will have to keep in mind that later Christian thought needed this concept to support various arguments for the existence of God, though not a God who has all the attributes you studied above.

So, while not rejecting these Greek concepts, you will see that any comparison with the Jewish concept you are exploring is very difficult. The interesting thing by way of comparison, though, is that both Greek and Jewish ideas about God are built into the foundations of our modern understanding of the divine. For now you need to be able to take the two ideas and contrast them. So the way the Jewish God is seen as intimately involved with creation in a loving and sustaining way will need to be explored. It may also be worth comparing the characteristics we attribute to God with the two different accounts of God's nature you are examining.

So what would be the same in their differing attitudes to God? The most obvious part of this answer is that God or the Prime Mover are both seen as responsible for the world, though you may wish to unpack the extent to which one view is deist and the other is a much more theist view. One way of looking at this is found in the film *Oh, God*, where George Burns, playing God, says: 'Think of me as being responsible for the big picture – the details are up to you.'

You could then go on to to look at the differences, exploring, for example, whether the terms 'omnipotent', 'omniscient' or 'omnipresent' would have meant anything to Aristotle. Aristotle's God may need to be all-powerful but would he care to be everywhere or know everything?

This should lead you to a discussion of the fundamental difference in the world view between the Greeks and the Jews. The Jewish writers, for example, never question whether or not there is a God; they are merely discussing the type of God revealed to them and the nature of mankind's relationship with that God. This may lead you to examine the beliefs of a nation who believed they were specially chosen to be the children of Yahweh as opposed to a more rationalistic approach found in the writings of Aristotle.

Exercises and Examination Advice

Make a list of the following terms in your notes and make sure you research them until you have a clear understanding of what each means:

God as Creator

God as Craftsman

Omnipotence

Omniscience

Omnipresence

God as Good

God as Lawgiver

God as Judge

God as the Source of Human Ethics

Creatio ex nihilo

Prime Mover

There are several different concepts you have to be aware of in this chapter so that, once again, you will be able to select the most relevant information for any given question. Above you have an account of the comparison which can be made between Aristotle's Prime Mover and the Jewish understanding of their Creator God. So the phrase 'creatio ex nihilo' may be a good alternative exercise.

If you are going to be clear about what this concept means in your answer, you may want to be able to explore the history of this idea and be able to describe the debate about its origins. For example, which scholars see this concept either implicitly or explicitly as present in the book of Genesis? To what extent did the Gnostics influence the growth of this belief? Why did the Fathers of the fourth Lateran Council make it a statement of their Church's belief?

It may therefore be good to work on the following question:

a. **Describe the meaning of the concept *creatio ex nihilo*. [25]**

b. **'Creation from nothing is impossible.' Discuss. [10]**

Notes

1. John Polkinghorne (1994) *Science and Christian Belief* (London: SPCK), p. 71.
2. Jeremiah 18.6 (New Jerusalem Bible).
3. Isaiah 64.7 (New Jerusalem Bible).
4. Malachi 3.3 (New Jerusalem Bible).
5. Augustine, *Confessions* 11.5.7.
6. Medieval Sourcebook: Twelfth Ecumenical Council: Lateran IV 1215.

The Ontological Argument 5

Introduction

Few arguments in the history of Philosophy have produced as much debate as this famous argument. Some philosophers still support versions of the argument – a new formulation was suggested in Professor David Smith's inaugural lecture at the University of Sussex – while other thinkers find little merit in it. Many of the opponents have offered alternative reasons for believing in God. It is valuable to know this: just because you may believe in God, it does not follow that you are committed to accepting any particular argument for his existence – as a scholar and philosopher, your concern is about whether a given argument establishes the conclusion it claims to reach.

The key feature of the argument, in all its forms, is that it is *a priori* (see Chapter 1 – The Basics), claiming that the very definition of God necessarily entails his existence, just as the definition of a square necessarily entails having four sides. But the obvious question to think about is whether we can go from a definition to a fact about the universe. Just because squares have four sides, by definition, does not mean that squares exist, just as we cannot say that because a mermaid is by definition half-woman, half-fish, that mermaids must therefore exist. Bear this point in mind as you consider the argument.

St Anselm's Version of the Argument

St Anselm of Canterbury (1033–1109) was one of the greatest thinkers of the medieval period. He was aware of the logic of Aristotle which he knew about, second-hand, from the commentaries of Boethius. As we shall see, he makes use of Boethius in his argument.

St Anselm came from Aosta in Northern Italy, and became a monk, joining the great abbey at Bec, in Normandy. He rose to be prior, second in importance after the abbot, and responsible for the day-to-day running of the monastery. In 1066, the Duke of Normandy, William the Conqueror, invaded England and installed Lanfranc, abbot of Bec, another Italian, as Archbishop of Canterbury. Anselm became abbot. Lanfranc died in 1089. The King of England, William II (William Rufus) was not interested in religion, but, after pressure, appointed Anselm Archbishop of Canterbury in 1093. The relationship with William was fractious, and bad relations continued between Anselm and Henry I after William's mysterious death (by an arrow of unknown origin) in the New Forest in 1100.

His Ontological Argument (the title was not his, but was given in the eighteenth century by Immanuel Kant) may be found in his very brief work, *Proslogion*, written while at Bec. St Anselm believed that true understanding was a consequence of faith – his personal motto was *Credo ut intelligam* (I believe that I may understand). The entire book is cast as a prayer. Anselm's intention is twofold: to demonstrate that God exists, the subject of Chapter Two, and then, in subsequent chapters, to demonstrate that God is indeed the type of God in whom Christians believe.

As an exercise in reading, and to demonstrate the value of following work as closely as possible, we have produced a new and very literal translation of Anselm. Read Chapter Two separately from Chapter Three: they are separate arguments.

The Ontological Argument

Chapter Two

<u>That God Truly Is</u>

Therefore, O Lord, who gives to faith understanding, give to me, as far as you know it to be expedient, that I may understand that

you exist, as we believe, and

you are what we believe you are

And, indeed, we believe you are something than which nothing greater can be thought.

Or is there no such nature, as the fool has said in his heart: 'There is no God.'

But certainly that very fool, when he hears what I now say: 'something than which nothing greater can be thought', understands what he hears

and what he hears is in his understanding,

even though he does not understand it to exist.

Now, there is a difference between a thing's being in the understanding and its being understood to exist.

For when the painter thinks ahead to that [the painting] which is to be made, he truly has it in his understanding, but does not yet understand to exist that which he has not yet made.

When, however, he has made the painting, he has in his understanding *and* understands to exist that which he has now made.

So even the fool is therefore bound to admit that there at least exists in his understanding something than which nothing greater can be thought, because

when he hears this he understands, and

whatever is understood is in the understanding.

And certainly, that than which a greater cannot be thought is not possible to be in the understanding alone,

for if it is at least in the understanding alone, it can be thought also to exist in fact, and this is more great.

For this reason, if that than which a greater cannot be thought is in the understanding only, then

the very thing than which a more great is *not* able to be thought is that than which a more great *is* able to be thought.

But obviously, this [contradiction] cannot be.

So, therefore, without any doubt, that than which a more great is not able to be thought exists both in the understanding and in fact.

Chapter Three

That he cannot be thought not to be

Which indeed is so true that it is *not possible* for it **to be thought** *not to be.*

Because something is *possible* **to be thought** *to be* which is *not possible* **to be thought** *not to be,*

and the latter is greater than that which is *possible* **to be thought** *not to be.*

Wherefore, if that than which a greater cannot be thought is *possible* **to be thought** *not to be*, then

the very thing than which a greater cannot be thought is *not* that than which a greater cannot be thought;

but this cannot be consistent.

So real therefore is the thing than which nothing greater can be thought that it is not even able to be thought not to be.

And this is what you are, O Lord our God.

Therefore, so truly do you exist, O Lord my God, that you are not even able to be thought not to be.

And rightly so, because if a mind could think of something better than you, the creature would rise above the creator, and would judge the creator, which is the height of absurdity. And truly, whatever else exists, apart from you alone, can be thought not to exist, because anything else does not exist so truly, and therefore has less being.

Why therefore has the fool said in his heart 'God is not', when it is obvious to the rational mind that you have being in the highest degree? Why, unless he is stupid and a fool?

The argument of Chapter Two is relatively straightforward, and is based on the logical impossibility of a contradiction. St Anselm is referring to the fool in the Psalms who says in his heart that there is no God. What Anselm then does is to offer a definition which, he claims, the fool himself will accept, that God is indeed 'something than which nothing greater can be thought'. He differentiates between things in the understanding and those which are understood to exist. For example, I understand what a mermaid is – I have the idea of a mermaid in my understanding, but it is not my understanding that mermaids actually exist as beings in the world. This is the point Anselm makes about the painter. Before he paints the picture, the idea is in his understanding, but he does not think it exists – he thinks that only when he has painted it. That is the position of the Fool – he knows the definition of God, but he does not think that there is in the world something equivalent to the definition.

But, says Anselm, he is contradicting himself. If God is the greatest thing we can think of *and* he does not exist, he would not be the greatest thing we can think of, as a real thing is greater – being more real – than something that does not exist. As we have seen in Chapter One, a contradiction is impossible, so, thinks Anselm, God must exist.

Chapter Three concerns the first quality of God: that it is not even possible for him to be thought not to exist. This is often interpreted to mean that God is a *necessary* being, one who has to exist, unlike *contingent* beings, like ourselves, who might or might not exist – if our parents had not met, for instance, we would not be here. Contingent beings depend on other things for their existence. This interpretation is limited – Anselm is going further than this. You will notice that we have done something funny to the print in our translation, to bring out Anselm's reliance on Boethius.

Boethius, in his Commentary on Aristotle's *Categories*, argues that everything that we can think of comes into one or more of four categories:

- Possible to be
- Possible not to be
- Not possible to be
- Not possible not to be

Now you and I – and gerbils and daffodils and most things around us – fall into the first two categories, which means they are contingent. Square circles are impossible, thus falling into the third category. The fourth category is necessary beings, things that have to be. If you look back at Chapter Three of *Proslogion*, you will see that the language of the categories is there, but you will notice the addition of 'to be thought' in every usage. In St Anselm's day, scientists thought necessary beings included all permanent things, which, to them, included the earth, the sun, the stars and so on. They were created by God, but as necessary beings. What Anselm is doing is to show, using the same pattern of argument as Chapter Two, that God is not simply another necessary being, but even more significant – he alone cannot even be thought not to exist. (You will find the language of Boethius recurring in the Third of Aquinas' Five Ways in the next chapter.)

Gaunilo's Criticism and St Anselm's Response

Gaunilo of Marmoutiers, another monk and contemporary of St Anselm, thought there was something wrong with the argument. He wrote a short book, *In Behalf of the Fool*. His argument was that St Anselm's argument was an exercise in wishful thinking, in that it permitted anything to be thought into existence. Consider the Perfect Island. If the Perfect Island did not exist, it would be a contradiction to call it the Perfect Island. Therefore it, and the perfect whatever else we may think of, must exist. This is absurd. The Perfect Island does not exist. If parallel arguments are absurd then the original is absurd.

St Anselm wrote a response, pointing out that an island is contingent. Its existence is contingent; that is, it depends on things like sea and earth. Islands do not have to exist, so their existence cannot be necessary. He might have added that the idea of the perfect island does not make sense – it is undefinable. If I add one grain of sand, does it become imperfect? Is a perfect island plus a hundred extra grains even more perfect? And, if we keep adding billions of grains, it ceases to be a perfect island and becomes Australia, instead. When does an island become a continent?

In Chapter Nine of his reply, St Anselm gives an important further clarification. The verb he uses throughout the argument is *intelligere*, that is, 'to understand'. It is not merely that the concept of God needs to be thought – it needs to be really understood. That is why, at the end of Chapter Three, Anselm says that the fool says what he does because he has not really understood the thought he had.

Aquinas

In his *Summa Theologicae* (I, q.2, a.1, c), St Thomas Aquinas would add his own objection:

> A thing can be self-evident in either of two ways: on the one hand, self-evident in itself, though not to us; on the other, self-evident in itself and to us. A proposition is self-evident because the predicate is included in the essence of the subject: *e.g., Man is an animal*, because 'animal' is contained in the essence of 'man'. . . . If . . . there are some to whom the essence of the predicate and the subject is unknown, the proposition will be self-evident in itself, but not to those ignorant of the meaning of the subject and predicate of the proposition. Therefore, as Boethius says, there are some concepts which are common and self-evident only to the learned, *e.g.* . . . *Incorporeal substances are not in space*. Therefore, I say that the proposition *God exists* is in itself self-evident, because God is his own essence . . . [But] because we do not know the essence of God, the proposition is not self-evident to us, but must be demonstrated by things that are more known to us, though less evident in themselves – namely, by his effects.

Aquinas argues here that something is self-evident in two ways – for us we need to be able to see the self-evidence, and we simply lack evidence of God to be able to understand the full meaning of the proposition. An easy way to understand this is to think of an English sentence such as 'A square has four sides.' That is self-evidently true to me, but would not be self-evident to someone who spoke no English. One has to be in the right place to see the self-evidence. Notice, by the way, how Aquinas uses Boethius to argue against Anselm. He often uses philosophers' own sources to argue against them.

As we shall see, Aquinas, as a good Aristotelian, would go on to base his own arguments for the existence of God on observed features of the world.

Descartes

In the later Middle Ages, discussion tended to focus on the arguments of St Thomas. But the Ontological Argument took on a new lease of life in the work of René Descartes (1596–1650). Descartes is a key figure in the history of mathematics as well as in philosophy. He is sometimes described as the Father of Modern Philosophy.

Perhaps the key work for present discussion is his *Meditations*. This is a curious, very readable (and mercifully short) book, with no very technical language. Descartes attempts to reconstruct all knowledge from first principles. Finding himself with nothing better to do, he shut himself in a stove-heated room to ask the question whether there was any knowledge so certain that no one could doubt it. Immediately he had to doubt the evidence of his senses. After all, we have no independent check that what our senses tell us is real. Descartes speculated that perhaps what we think to be real is simply a malicious demon making us imagine a world. (In modern times, Hilary Putnam considered whether we might just be brains in laboratory vats, having electrical impulses in those brains manipulated to think we were full beings moving about.)

Descartes considered that there was at least one certain piece of knowledge – *cogito, ergo sum* – I think, therefore I am. He was, of course, mistaken. Firstly, 'I think, therefore I am' is not certain as it is not a tautology: 'existing' is not a necessary part of the definition of thinking. Secondly, we cannot go from 'there is a thought now' to the connected person I mean by the word 'I'. 'I' indicates someone with past, present and future. How do I know the memories I think I have are not the work of that malicious demon? In any case, Descartes' systematic doubt does not include the origin and meaning of the language in which he frames his questions. Does not the meaning of language presuppose a degree of relationship (just what is much argued by philosophers) with the world to give sense to the words we use? No less plausibly, we might suggest that if one asks a silly question, one should not be surprised by a silly answer. Nothing is as real to me as I am to myself – it cannot be as I cannot experience the not-me in the way I experience myself. Think about this. If I ask whether the Loch Ness Monster is real, or ghosts are real, I am not asking whether they are real in the way that I am to myself. I am asking whether they are real objects in the world as chairs or tables or gerbils are. 'Real' is a relative term, in that to ask if something is real is to ask whether it is as real as . . . . . . (please fill in the blank). Aristotle and Aquinas treated objects in the world – Being – as the benchmark of reality. This is closer to the ordinary language approach.

The relevance of this to God is twofold. Firstly, it raises important questions about what it means to say 'God is real'. The one thing about God, if he exists, is that his reality would be nothing like mine or that of an object in the world. Secondly, it creates an important question for Descartes. He wants to prove that the objects of the world are much as we perceive them. He cannot do this directly, as he cannot use the evidence of his senses, given his initial doubt about sense experience. But another route is possible. If he could demonstrate that God existed, then he could argue that God does not play tricks on us, and that therefore the world is pretty much as we think it is. But he cannot rely on sense experience to give evidence of God, for reasons we have seen. He has to find an *a priori* proof which demonstrates that God has to exist – an Ontological Argument.

Scholars question whether Descartes knew of St Anselm's argument. When asked by friends, Descartes appears to have mumbled that he ought to look it up. Where his argument is similar, it is in being *a priori* and its assumption that existence is intrinsic to the definition of God.

Descartes builds his arguments on two notions:

- God is by definition perfect. An imperfect God would not be God. So, if God is perfect, he must contain all perfections, including the perfection of existence. If he did not exist he would not be perfect. So, he must exist.
- Existence is a defining predicate of the concept of God in exactly the same way that having three sides and three angles is intrinsic to the concept of a triangle. Without three sides there can be no concept of a triangle. Remember that a defining predicate is a description something has to have to be itself. It is essentially tautologous – Kant uses the term 'analytic' for a sentence of this type.

Kant's Objections

In the *Critique of Pure Reason*, Kant develops two criticisms of Descartes – these also have force against St Anselm's version of the argument:

- Suppose Descartes is right and existence is indeed a defining predicate of the concept of God. There is no contradiction – and hence no impossibility – in rejecting a concept together with all its defining predicates. To take an earlier example, I can accept that being half-woman and half-fish is a defining predicate of the idea of a mermaid. I would not be contradicting myself if I said I did not believe in mermaids or creatures who were half-woman and half-fish. I would only be talking nonsense, and contradicting myself, if I said I believed mermaids existed but rejected creatures who were half-woman and half fish, or vice versa. In the same way, I could say that I accepted that if God existed then he would necessarily exist, but that I did not believe in him or in his necessary existence. There would be no contradiction here.
- Kant's second objection is based on the belief that existence is not a predicate at all, and therefore cannot be a defining predicate. Remember that a predicate adds a description to a concept. So, if I say, 'the square is red', or 'my cat is tabby', the 'is red' or the 'is tabby' tells us something about the idea of the square or the idea of my cat. But when I say 'x exists', I am not adding anything to the *concept* of x: instead, I am asserting that in the real world there exists an object which corresponds to the concept 'x'. Think about this for a moment. Suppose I believe in the existence of mermaids and you do not. There is actually no difference between us about what a mermaid might be: we agree that it would be half-woman, half-fish, and so on. What we differ about is not the idea of the mermaid, but whether something just like the mermaid-concept could be found out there in the real world. Our *concept* of the mermaid is as near-identical, perhaps as wholly identical, as may

be. So, if Kant is right, to say something exists adds nothing at all to the concept. Kant illustrates this point with the example of the conceptual difference between a hundred real and a hundred imaginary *thalers* – a common currency in Middle Europe at the time. In Frege–Russellian logical language, existence is shown as a quantifier, called the existential quantifier, not as a predicate. Take two sentences: 'The dragon breathes fire' and 'I am a philosopher'. They both look like concepts of the same type – a subject with a predicate. But there is an important difference. In the first case I do not think dragons really exist (cynic that I am!), whereas in the second I have good reasons for thinking I really do exist. Modern logical languages from Frege and Russell would express the difference like this:

a. *x* has the predicate *p* ['The dragon breathes fire']
b. (There exists *x*) (*x* has the predicate *p*) ['I am a philosopher']

That I exist may be the unspoken assumption of the second sentence, but it is there, though it is not a new description. The existence bit has a different function in the sentence.

STRETCH AND CHALLENGE

Immanuel Kant's dismissal of the Ontological Argument is based on his denial that necessary existence is a predicate or property of the concept of God. This leaves open the possibility of finding a new way of constructing the argument which avoids the claim that existence is a predicate. In the twentieth century, a new way forward appeared to be offered through the development of modal logic. Modal logic concerns the logic of possibility and necessity. Two versions of this revised Ontological Argument have been studied particularly closely – those of Norman Malcolm and Alvin Plantinga. There are other versions, such as that given by David Smith in his inaugural Professorial lecture at the University of Sussex.

Norman Malcolm (1911–90)

Malcolm's version of the argument ('Anselm's Ontological Argument'; *Philosophical Review*, vol. 69, no.1 (1960) pp. 41–62) is the simpler of the two, based on the idea of an unlimited being:

> God is usually conceived of as an *unlimited* being. He is conceived of as a being who *could not* be limited, that is as an absolutely unlimited being . . . If God is conceived to be an absolutely unlimited being He must be conceived to be unlimited in regard to His existence as well as His operation. In this conception it will not make sense to say that He depends on anything for coming into or continuing in existence. Nor, as Spinoza observed, will it make sense to say that something could *prevent* Him from existing. Lack of moisture can prevent trees from existing in a certain region of the earth. But it would be contrary to the concept of God as an unlimited being to suppose that anything . . . could prevent Him from existing.

From this, Malcolm deduces that God's existence cannot be contingent – it cannot causally depend on anything else.

The next step is the argument that the existence of an unlimited being is either logically necessary or logically impossible. Malcolm argues that an unlimited being is not logically impossible – something is only logically impossible if the concept is contradictory (e.g. a square circle is self-contradictory and logically impossible in all possible worlds). If unlimited being is not self-contradictory, it is not logically impossible. Thus we have the argument:

1. God is, as a matter of definition, an unlimited being.
2. The existence of an unlimited being is either logically necessary or logically impossible.
3. The existence of an unlimited being is not logically impossible.
4. Therefore, the existence of God is logically necessary.

The evident weakness of this argument lies in premise 2. It is not clear that logical necessity (which is a matter of definition) necessarily entails factual existence. More fatal to the argument is whether the concept of 'unlimited being' is coherent. Many views of God – including those of Process Theologians – suggest the possibility of limits on his foreknowledge, and serious questions have been asked by philosophers such as C. D. Broad on the compossibility of all the divine attributes. Christianity has traditionally spoken of the self-limitation of God, in order to give mankind the epistemic space to work out his own destiny. Michael Durrant, in his *Theology and Intelligibility* (1973), questions whether it makes sense to talk of God at all in substance terms, which would include thinking of him as a being.

Alvin Plantinga (1932–)

Plantinga's version of the Ontological Argument attempts to avoid the problems raised by a concept of unlimited being, preferring instead to develop his argument on the basis of two properties – *maximal excellence* and *maximal greatness*. He defines these as follows:

1. A being is *maximally excellent* if and only if [iff] it is omnipotent, omniscient and morally perfect in W [a possible world]; and
2. A being is *maximally great* in a world W iff it is maximally excellent in every possible world.

This idea is based on the assumption that the concept of a maximally great being is not self-contradictory. Logically, the only things that don't exist in any possible world are self-contradictory concepts – a square circle cannot exist in any possible world as the property of being circular is inconsistent with being square. Taking this, Plantinga constructs his argument on these lines:

1. The concept of a maximally great being is self-consistent.
2. If 1 is true, then there is at least one logically possible world in which a maximally great being exists.
3. If a maximally great being exists in one logically possible world, it exists in every logically possible world.
4. Therefore, a maximally great being (i.e. God) exists in every logically possible world.

Some philosophers have attempted to attack premise 3 on the grounds that it is based on an axiom of one system of modal logic (S5) which is not shared in other systems. The point here is this. Any logical language, as we saw in Chapter One, is a system of axioms – of rules. Change the rules and you create a new logical language. Logical languages are graded according to strength – *S1, S2, S3*, and so on. The lower the number, the fewer the axioms which make up the system. The axiom that comes into play at *S5* is the notion, familiar from mathematics, that two negatives make a positive:

$-- x = x$

Exactly the same notion is found in traditional systems of logic:

$$\sim\sim p \equiv p$$

You will recall that versions of the argument rest on a double negative. It assumes:

not possible not to be $\equiv$ must be

Surely, it is argued, to be accepted as certain, an axiom must hold in every possible system. If it does not, can we hold that it is a certain truth? Others have offered defences of the premise on grounds other than S5 axioms.

A much more potent attack is one based on the assumption of axiom 1. Is the concept of a maximally great being coherent? Notice Plantinga's idea that maximal excellence entails moral perfection. Some argue, for instance, that moral perfection implies being both perfectly merciful and perfectly just; but can God be both without self-contradiction? Perfect justice implies giving each person precisely what he deserves, neither more nor less; but perfect mercy implies giving each person less punishment than he deserves. The two seem inconsistent. Others draw attention to contradictions between divine foreknowledge and the possibility of genuine freewill.

An interesting approach could be developed on the basis of the Thomist belief that we are not in a position to know the essence of God (*S.T.* I, q.2, a.1, c), and therefore we cannot make the kinds of assumptions found in both Plantinga and Malcolm on the nature of God's attributes. Supporters of the apophatic way, otherwise known as *via negativa*, would argue that we can define God only in negative terms, as his greatness is so far beyond human imagination to encompass or human words to express. As a result, the kind of definition offered in these arguments is beyond human understanding. After all, Plantinga himself qualifies his argument by saying that he is demonstrating the logical possibility of God rather than offering a proof of his existence. He argues:

An argument for the existence of God may be *sound*, after all, without in any sense proving God's existence. . . . What I claim for this argument, therefore, is that it establishes, not the *truth* of theism, but its rational acceptability.[1]

Exercises and Examination Advice

Make a list of the following terms in your notes and make sure you research them until you have a clear understanding of what each means:

Syllogistic Logic

Ontological

True and valid arguments

Contingent existence

Necessary existence

Perfection in the Cartesian sense

Predicate

It is also important that you make good summary notes on the relevant writings of the following philosophers:

Anselm

Descartes

Gaunilo

Kant

This is clearly a very important part of the course as this way of thinking can be very different from anything you have tried before. It is worth taking the time to fully understand the way that this kind of logic works. In your answers you may, for example, be asked to be clear about why an argument like this could be valid but still untrue. If you do want to say why it is untrue then you would need to be clear about how the propositions lead to a valid conclusion which is to your mind not true.
    Take for example the simple syllogistic argument:

All fire engines are red.

This is a Fire Engine.

It must be red.

Anyone in the armed services could immediately tell you that while this may be a valid argument, it is untrue as services fire engines are green.
    I would think that it would be worth spending some time in class making your own arguments and testing them for truth and validity.
    After this exercise I would suggest you try making a list of the kind of things that have necessary or contingent existence; some examples may start some good classroom debates. A good debate is a better preparation for examination than learning essays by heart. I always remember the lecturer at my university who told us, '*You will never forget why you lose an argument and you will not try that route again.*'
    Finally you could try the following question:

a. **Explain the concept of 'necessary existence' as applied to a divine creator. [25]**

b. **'All existence is contingent'. Discuss. [10]**

Note

1. Alvin Plantinga (1977) *God, Freedom and Evil* (Grand Rapids: Eerdmans), p. 112.

St Thomas Aquinas and the Cosmological Argument

6

Introduction

More nonsense is written about the medieval period than about perhaps any period in history. For many, it is still seen as something of an intellectual desert between the high periods of ancient times and the intellectual revolutions marked by the Renaissance and the Reformation. Post-Reformation myths still abound. Two of the most common are that in the Middle Ages, monks spent their time trying to determine how many angels could dance on the head of a pin (something first mentioned long after the Middle Ages) or, even more commonly, that in those times everyone thought the earth was flat. Nothing is further from the truth. The error of medieval astronomers was to assume that the earth was at the centre of the universe, and, following Ptolemy's *Almagest*, that its circumference was smaller than it actually was. But all their astronomy shows that the earth was round.

The Middle Ages were a time of change. Technologically, enormous advances were made, in the development of animal power, through effective harnesses, which in turn improved transport of goods and, above all, ploughing, which meant improved agriculture. Developments in glass manufacture brought new lenses, the development of spectacles, wonderful coloured glass, and, crucial for the development of chemistry, heatproof glass for experiments. Chemicals were better refined, double-entry book-keeping enabled banking and easier trade, the use of Arabic figures enabled strides to be made in mathematics, while thinkers like Robert Grosseteste, Duns Scotus and William of Ockham laid the foundations of experimental method. Immense progress was made in medicine in terms of diagnosis.

Central to many of these developments was the reintroduction of Aristotle's works to Europe, not only in logic, but also in physics and biology. Though many of his scientific views have subsequently been shown to be wrong, his emphasis on careful observation, recording and categorizing of data gave science crucial impetus. In thought, there were many men of immense erudition, but a remarkable genius would attempt to think through in new ways the implications of Aristotle for philosophy and theology.

St Thomas Aquinas (1224/5–74) was one of the greatest philosophers of all time. His output was, as we shall see, astonishing, not merely in the sheer number of words produced, but in the range of topics he discussed. When asked towards the end of his life what was the greatest gift God had given him, he replied that he had never read a page he had not at once understood, yet the monk who heard his final confession left his room saying he had just heard the confession of a little child. This huge, very quiet man remains the focus of a vast literature.

Aquinas was born at Roccasecca, near Aquino, in Italy. He was of aristocratic back-ground, and studied at the great Benedictine monastery of Monte Cassino, before entering the University of Naples. He was nine years old. While at Naples he decided he wanted to join the new Order of Preachers, the Dominicans. His family had other ideas – the wanted him to become a Benedictine monk, perhaps to become Abbot at Monte Cassino. For a while they imprisoned him, but eventually he was able to fulfil his wish. (Notice that Aquinas was a Dominican, and hence a friar – not a monk. Monks commit themselves to a monastery, to live there probably for the rest of their lives. Aquinas committed himself to the Order, to live and work wherever they instructed him.) He went to Cologne, where he was a pupil of St Albert the Great (Albertus Magnus, c.1200–80). St Albert's intention was to provide a systematic account of the newly discovered and translated work of Aristotle, using it to interpret Christian thought. When Albert moved to the University of Paris, Aquinas followed. He began study for the degree of Master of Arts. Among the many tasks required was – as it would remain for several hundred years – to write a commentary on a fairly short theological text known as *The Sentences of Peter Lombard*. Aquinas' commentary ran to about 1,750,000 words. But he completed it before he was 30, so only the Pope could grant him the degree of master. That thesis established his reputation as the finest mind in Europe. Thereafter, his output was prodigious. He died in Fossanuova in Italy, but is buried in Toulouse, in France. He wrote commentaries on all the major books of Aristotle and on other authors, including Boethius. Other works included many volumes on disputed topics as well as monographs on particular questions, hymns, prayers, masses and others. He is best known for his two great Summas, *Summa Contra Gentiles* and *Summa Theologicae*. The latter was unfinished at his death, but is a monumental attempt to rethink the whole of Christian Faith, question by question. It is from this work that the Five Ways are taken.

A Note on Reading Aquinas

You may often return to Aquinas and it is helpful to know how to read him. Examiners often read remarks attributed to Aquinas, such as that if evil exists, God cannot, which do not represent his own views, but those of others who disagree with him.

The *Summa Theologicae* is divided into three parts. The Second Part is further subdivided into Parts One and Two. Each part is then divided into questions, such as 'The Existence of God'. Each question is then subdivided into articles, which are subdivisions of the question. Each article then has the following order:

- **Objections** to Aquinas' views are listed first.
- **Contrary** – this gives arguments that others might make against the objections.
- **Corpus**, or body of the article, beginning 'I answer that . . .', in which Aquinas develops his own position.
- **Replies to the Objections**.

Aquinas also uses certain honorific terms when referring to others. For him, Aristotle is always *The Philosopher*, the Arabic Philosopher Averröes is *The Commentator*, St Paul is *The Apostle*, and St John, *The Evangelist*.

The Five Ways and the Cosmological Argument

In Part I of the *Summa Theologicae*, Aquinas gives, in Question 2, Article 3, his famous Five Ways for the existence of God. In Article 1, he had, as we have seen, rejected the Ontological Argument, on the grounds that we cannot use an argument that God's existence is self-evident, as we cannot see that self-evidence. He argued that we need to argue to God from evidence that we find in the world. This is very Aristotelian – Aristotle always begins from observed features of the world. The first Three Ways are collectively known as the 'Cosmological' Argument. In Aquinas' words:

[PRIME MOVER[1]] The first and most obvious way is the argument from motion. It is obvious that in the world some things are in motion. Whatever is moved is moved by another . . . It is impossible that in the same respect and in the same way a thing could be both mover and moved, *i.e.*, that it should move itself. Whatever is moved is moved by another. If that by which it is moved is itself moving, then this must also be moved by something else, and that by something else again. But this cannot go on to infinity, because there would then be no first mover, and, consequently, no subsequent mover, as subsequent movers move only insofar as they are moved by the first mover, just as a staff moves only because it is moved by the hand. So there must be a first mover, itself unmoved; and this everyone understands to be God.

[FIRST CAUSE] The second way is from the nature of efficient causes. In the world of sensible things we find an order of efficient causes. There is no case known (it would be impossible) in which a thing is found to be its own efficient cause; to be so it would have to exist prior to itself, which is impossible. In efficient causes we cannot go on to infinity, because in any order of efficient causes, the first is the cause of the intermediate and the intermediate of the last, whether there are several intermediate causes or only one. Without a cause, there is no effect. Thus, if there were no first cause . . . there would be no intermediate causes, and no last. If we could go to infinity in efficient causes, there would be no first cause; if that were true, there would be no intermediate cause, and no present effects for us to see. Plainly this is not the case. So we must admit a first efficient cause [itself uncaused], which everyone calls 'God'.

[NECESSITY AND CONTINGENCY] The third way is taken from possibility and necessity. In nature we find things that are possible to be and not to be – they are found to be generated and corrupted – and so it is possible for them to be and possible not to be. It is impossible for them always to exist, for that which is possible not to be at some time does not exist. If everything is like that, at one time nothing existed. If that were true, there would be nothing in existence now, because things only come to exist because of things already existing. If at some time nothing existed, there would be nothing today, which is obviously false. So, not all things are merely possible – there must exist something whose existence is necessary. Every necessary thing either has its necessity caused by something else, or it does not. As we saw when we considered efficient causes, it would be impossible to go on to infinity in a chain of things which have their necessity caused by another necessary being. We have to admit the existence of some being whose necessity lies in itself (and not received from something else), which is the source of necessity in others. This all men call God.

If we read these arguments carefully, we recognize that the Prime Mover is based very obviously on Aristotle, and was dealt with in that chapter. For the moment, we will concentrate on the arguments from First Cause and Contingency and Necessity.

First Cause

This is a particularly appealing, but rather problematic, argument. It is the closest to the one we hear most commonly, which is when people ask, if there is no God, where did the universe come from? Cause is something we see all the time – everything is caused by something else, that in turn by something else, and so on. Surely, the argument says, there must be a first cause, different from the others in requiring no cause. It obviously makes no sense to ask the question, 'What Caused God?' The very term 'God' refers to something that does not have a cause – a caused God would be a contradiction in terms.

There are two particular difficulties:

- David Hume identified problems with the very notion of causation. We speak of cause and effect, and assume we understand the notion, but, scientifically, it remains problematic. Consider the moment when the cause is succeeded by the effect. Immediately before that moment, the cause is not yet the effect. Immediately after, the effect is no longer the cause. What happens in the precise moment when the cause is not yet the effect and the effect is no longer the cause? Science will tell us what went before, and what came after, but the moment itself remains a deep intellectual puzzle. The ease with which we talk of cause and effect disguises the complexity of the notion. Hume suggests that what we call 'cause and effect' may simply be our way of reporting what is just a statistical correlation. Instead of saying, 'x causes y', precisely the same phenomenon might be described by saying, 'whenever x, y'. In this case, we describe the phenomenon without any mention of cause.
- Whatever is meant by 'cause', in relation to God, cannot be cause in the ordinary scientific sense – God is not another cause in the way that my boot is the cause of a football's movement or the mixture of certain chemicals is the cause of the explosion which removed my eyebrows. If God is a cause, then he is a cause of a very different kind from anything in my experience, and I may properly ask on what evidence I can posit a cause of a type outside my experience, or, indeed, any earthly experience. I know what a biological cause, a chemical cause, might be: but I have no direct experience of divine cause, so am I able to posit it?

Some of these difficulties have been noted by Dorothy Emmet (1904–2000) in a book written towards the end of her life:

'First Cause' is not, I think, the first member of a causal sequence, although this is suggested in the Five Ways. . . . It is an eternal non-temporal activity on which everything else depends. 'Cause' is now recognised to be a problematic notion, even in its normal use. How much more so in this abnormal use?[2]

The problems mentioned by Hume and Emmet seem to afflict an argument, originally developed in the Islamic Kalam school of Philosophy. The American philosopher, William Lane Craig has made much of it. Nevertheless, it seems to exhibit many flaws. The key steps of the argument are:

1. Everything that begins to exist has a cause so that it can exist.
2. The universe began to exist.
3. Therefore, the Universe must have a cause for its existence.

The inference drawn by enthusiasts for this argument is that therefore God must be that cause.

The argument appears weak on every level. Premise 1 is not self-evidently true, nor can it be. Even if everything we itemized had a cause, we cannot *know* that everything has a cause – we cannot deduce the necessary *all* from many instances. Indeed, modern Physics suggests that there are uncaused events at the micro-particle level. One disconfirming instance is sufficient to overthrow the assertion of this major premise.

Premise 2 is an assumption. It is widely shared by many and seems implicit in the Big Bang Theory, but it is not a truth that is known. Aristotle thought the universe was without beginning and the idea of an infinite universe is not self-contradictory.

Premise 3 is open to the objections of Hume against causation. In any case, even if the universe had a cause, it is not legitimate to assume that cause to be God. That there *was* a cause does not demonstrate that that cause still exists, any more than that while, without my ancestors, I would not exist, it does not follow that my ancestors still exist so I can write this book. It does not follow from my living that my great grandfather is still pottering in the garden. And the cause that is being inferred would be something very different from any kind of cause, whether biological or physical, that we might ever experience.

Necessity and Contingency

In this argument we see clearly the influence of Boethius, as noted in our discussion of St Anselm's *Proslogion* 3 in the last chapter. Notice the recurrence of terms such as 'possible to be' and 'possible not to be'. Aquinas' argument, in essence, appears to be that everything in our experience is contingent, but not everything can be so contingent. There must be something necessary, not dependent on anything else, on which everything else depends.

The problem that most immediately occurs is Aquinas' assumption about a time when once there was nothing. There is no reason to assume that there need have been such a time. There could be overlapping chains of contingent beings, so that there never was a period when nothing existed. There is no logical impossibility in this – there is no contradiction intrinsic to the concept of an endless chain of contingent beings.

A further problem has been raised, among others by Bertrand Russell in his radio debate with Frederick Copleston (see next chapter). The question was whether it makes sense to speak of a 'necessary being'. In logic, a proposition may be described as 'necessary'. It is, for example, as we have seen, a necessary truth of language that a square has four sides. Tautologies are necessary truths, though, it will be recalled, they tell us nothing about the actual contents of the world. But can a thing be necessary? Whatever we mean here by the term 'necessary', it is a special usage. But, if nothing else than God is necessary, and we cannot see his necessity directly, it seems impossible to argue that we have any concept of necessary being that we can attribute as Aquinas does here.

The Appeal to Imagination

We should note again, as pointed out in the chapter on Aristotle, that this argument appeals to the alleged impossibility of an infinite regress. In *Mens Creatrix* the future Archbishop, William Temple, commented that '. . . it is impossible to imagine infinite regress . . . [but] it is not impossible to conceive it'.[3] What he meant by this is that something is unthinkable if we cannot hold the concept without contradiction. The concept of a square circle is inconceivable because the two words contradict each other. But 'infinite' does not contradict 'regress'. I cannot imagine infinity, but I can think of it – I know what the word means and I understand the idea. To say it is impossible for me to imagine something says something about the limits of human imagination, but not about the limitations of things: I cannot assume that because I cannot imagine four or five or six dimensions that I cannot think about the possibility. Indeed, mathematicians today, recognizing that mathematics is systems of definitions, quite happily do multidimensional geometry, even though they are quite unable to draw the diagrams, or even to imagine them.

Perhaps the Cosmological Argument could be rewritten to avoid some of these objections. Other formulations are the subject of our next chapter.

Exercises and Examination Advice

Make a list of the following terms in your notes and make sure you research them until you have a clear understanding of what each means:

Cosmological

Kalam Argument

Necessity

Contingency

It is also important that you make good summary notes on the relevant writings of the following philosophers:

Thomas Aquinas

Hume

Russell

Copleston

Terminology is very important in this kind of argument. I am often asked by my pupils why philosophers seem to say very simple things in unnecessarily complicated ways. The obvious answer, and the least helpful from their point of view, is that the complexity is not unnecessary. Twentieth-century British philosophers spent a great deal of their lives exploring what can and cannot be said meaningfully. You will look at this in more detail during the A2 course. For now, it is important that you learn to be very clear about exactly what any philosopher was trying to say.

You will notice that all of the arguments studied in this book were written by men of faith who were trying to see if this faith was rational. So here Aquinas is not looking to argue for the existence of the God of classical theism but merely a divine creator. So here you are exploring the extent to which the existence of God can be said to be factually necessary, not as Anselm attempted to prove his existence logically.

Try this:

a. **Explain the meaning of 'factually necessary existence'. [25]**

b. **'No existence is logically necessary.' Discuss. [10]**

Notes

1. The titles in square brackets refer to the titles by which these arguments are traditionally known. These titles were *not* given by St Thomas.
2. Dorothy Emmet (1998) *Outward Forms, Inner Springs* (Basingstoke: Macmillan), p. 71.
3. William Temple (1915) *Mens Creatrix* (London: Macmillan), p. 271.

The Cosmological Argument II – God as Explanation

Introduction

Given the problems of arguing for God as First Cause, Necessary Being or Prime Mover, many philosophers have preferred to argue in terms of God as Ultimate Explanation of the universe. A problem of arguments from Prime Mover or First Cause, casually understood, is that they appear, at least superficially, to be about the beginning of things – that there *was* a cause or mover, or, come to that, a designer. But most religious people see God's relationship with the world as one which is not a matter of beginning but of continual sustaining. The German-American theologian Paul Tillich (1886–1965) speaks of God as the 'Ground of Being'. Such an account talks of God in terms of continued action.

The modern turn has been perhaps to see God especially in terms of *explanation*, the idea that God alone explains what exists. Explanation is a concept which does not confine us simply to past events – explanation involves not only origins but intentions, plans, contingency and so on.

The concept was developed in the work of the great German philosopher and mathematician, Gottfried Wilhelm Leibniz (1646–1716). An important part of his thought was that the universe is a harmonious whole, which is essentially good. God created this world for a particular reason as the best of all possible worlds. (This view of Leibniz is savagely satirized by Voltaire in *Candide*.) The reason God has is, in principle, intelligible to us. A key principle is the Principle of Sufficient Reason. As he says in *Monadology* (§53):

> As there is, in God's ideas, an infinity of possible universes, yet only one can exist, there has to be a sufficient reason for God's choice, a reason which makes him make one choice rather than a different one.

This assumes that the universe is in principle rational and open to human intelligence to understand. Such a notion underlies all attempts to see God as explanation.

It is an understandable assumption, though, as we shall see, it raises many questions. After all, it is the practice of scientists, on coming upon a strange phenomenon, not to hold up their hands and to be satisfied by saying 'It's a mystery!' Science works on the assumption that there is an explanation for all phenomena, and thus that they are, in principle at least, capable of finding it. If each individual phenomenon is explicable, is it not reasonable to ask whether the whole universe has an explanation? As we shall see, the assumption involved here is a large one.

But not all views of explanation are necessarily scientific. There is something which is called Personal Explanation, where something is not the result of a sequence of causes but the result of choice. There are physical reasons for the existence of this book, but the main reason is that certain people chose to write it. That is the key explanation, to which the physical reasons for its being here are real but secondary. In recent years, Richard Swinburne has developed many aspects of this idea of personal explanation in his books on the existence of God and in many conference addresses. Perhaps the strongest example of this way of thinking can be found in extracts from William Temple:

> When in the causal regress we arrive at a will, the regress is at an end, and to understand means, not to give a causal explanation, but to sympathise. We have reached an ultimate term. And when we do sympathise, our mind raises no more questions. The only explanation of the Universe that would really explain it, in the sense of providing an answer that raises no further question, would be the demonstration that it is the creation of a Will which in the creative act seeks an intelligible good. But that is Theism.[1]

> . . . when we turn from the world as apprehended by Mind to Mind which apprehends the World, we find among its functions a principle which is self-explanatory – the principle of Purpose or of Intelligent Choice. This is an ultimate principle of explanation. When we find that the position of a given set of material objects is due to their having been arranged with a view to facilitating the accomplishment of some intelligible purpose, our minds are satisfied. That a plank should lie across a stream may call for much explanation if no human beings have ever placed it there; but if men laid it across to form a bridge, so that they could cross over dry-shod, no further explanation is needed. Purpose is a self-explanatory principle.[2]

The obvious problem here is that Temple's view presumes a satisfaction theory of truth, that is, it assumes that we have discovered the truth when we are satisfied. But whether or not I am satisfied is a matter of my psychology. If asked why leaves fall off trees in autumn, someone might say, 'Because leaves are like that.' Someone might be satisfied by the answer, but it is not a satisfactory answer, because someone else might ask many more questions, beginning with, 'Why are they like that?' To say that *because* my mind is satisfied, I have discovered truth, seems presumptuous. People are, after all, satisfied or not with the oddest reasoning. Consider an event such as the deaths of President Kennedy or Diana, Princess of Wales. There are those satisfied by the official theories, of lone assassin or drunken driver. There are those who argue in each case that there had to be some kind of conspiracy which is being covered up. It sometimes seems as if for some people, only a conspiracy theory can ever be sufficient explanation. But it is no guarantee that the theory is the right one.

The Copleston–Russell Debate

The Jesuit philosopher, Father Frederick Copleston (1907–94), better known as F. C. Copleston, Professor of the History of Philosophy at the University of London, was involved in two very significant Third Programme debates for BBC radio. The one that interests us at present is his debate with Bertrand Russell in 1948 (the other was with A. J. Ayer in 1949) on the existence of God. Bertrand Russell (1872–1970) was, as we have seen in Chapter One, crucial to the development of modern logic, but distinguished also in fields such as epistemology and a prolific commentator on a variety of matters including pacifism (for which he was imprisoned more than once) and religion. His *Why I am not a Christian* remains one of his most read works.

Their debate, allegedly fuelled by a shared bottle of whisky provided in advance by a BBC producer, is remarkably wide-ranging, including discussion about whether it makes sense to speak of God as a necessary being, a topic touched on in our chapter on the Ontological Argument. Additionally, there is a valuable passage about whether morality is evidence for God. The whole debate is easily available on the internet and we would strongly recommend you to read or listen to it.[3]

Copleston argues for a version of the Cosmological Argument, drawing heavily on Leibniz's Principle of Sufficient Reason. He says:

I'll divide the argument into distinct stages. First of all, I should say, we know that there are at least some beings in the world which do not contain in themselves the reason for their existence. For example, I depend on my parents, and now on the air, and on food, and so on. Now, secondly, the world is simply the real or imagined totality or aggregate of individual objects, none of which contain in themselves alone the reason for their existence. There isn't any world distinct from the objects which form it, any more than the human race is something apart from the members. Therefore, I should say, since objects or events exist, and since no object of experience contains within itself reason of its existence, this reason, the totality of objects, must have a reason external to itself. That reason must be an existent being. Well, this being is either itself the reason for its own existence, or it is not. If it is, well and good. If it is not, then we must proceed farther. But if we proceed to infinity in that sense, then there's no explanation of existence at all. So, I should say, in order to explain existence, we must come to a being which contains within itself the reason for its own existence, that is to say, which cannot not exist.

Notice that he talks of reason and explanation, not of cause. When Russell checks this, Copleston says that cause may be a reason, but that 'by sufficient reason in the full sense I mean an explanation adequate for the existence of some particular being. . . . An adequate explanation must ultimately be a total explanation, to which nothing further can be added.' His argument is that the universe must have a meaning, arguing that things in the universe are explicable, that science works on that assumption, and that it is reasonable to assume that therefore the whole universe has an explanation.

Russell points to the incidence of uncaused – and hence, in principle unexplainable – beings in the universe, citing individual quantum transitions in atoms as examples. Copleston also mentions indeterminacy, but does not see this as damaging his argument.

At the centre of Russell's case is the simple statement that 'I should say that the universe is just there, and that's all.' It is a brute fact, not itself capable of, or requiring, any further explanation.

Behind Russell's argument is the awareness of a logical fallacy, known as 'The Fallacy of Composition'. This fallacy is the assumption that because something is true of the parts, it must be true of the whole. (Aristotle is perhaps guilty of this error when he argues that because every part of the body has a function, man as a whole must also have a function.) Russell once suggested that we cannot go from saying that all mankind has a mother to the assumption that the universe has. He is also, perhaps, pointing to a psychological fact – we may wish there to be an explanation, just as we always want reasons, but we cannot go from our desire for something to the assumption that therefore that something must exist. We cannot assert that there *must* be an explanation unless we have some evidence that there *is* an explanation. But that is precisely the point at issue.

Criticisms of the Debate

An interesting criticism of Russell's position is offered by the Dominican philosopher, Herbert McCabe (1926–2001):

. . . of course it is always possible to stop the questioning at any point; a man may refuse to ask why there are dogs. He may say there just *are* dogs and perhaps it is impious to ask how come – there were people who actually said that to Darwin. Similarly it is possible to refuse to ask this ultimate question, to say as Russell once did: the universe is just there. This seems to me just as arbitrary as to say: dogs are just there. The difference is that we now know by hindsight that Darwin's critics were irrational because we have familiarised ourselves with an *answer* to the question, how come there are dogs? We have not familiarised ourselves with the answer to the question, how come the world instead of nothing? But that does not make it any less arbitrary to refuse to ask it. To ask it is to enter on an exploration which Russell was simply refusing to do, as it seems to me. It is of course perfectly right to point out the mysteriousness of a question about *everything*, to point to the fact we have no way of answering it, but that is by no means the same as saying it is an unaskable question. As Wittgenstein said, 'Not *how* the world is, but *that* it is, is the mystery.'[4]

Notice, however, that McCabe is simply defending the legitimacy of the question. He is himself cautious about the explanation, arguing that when we talk of explanation, we are stretching human concepts. He comments:

. . . we are asking our ultimate radical question with tools that will not do the job properly, with words whose meaning has to be stretched beyond what we can comprehend. It would be very strange if it were not so. . . . If the question of God were a neat and simple question to be answered in terms of familiar concepts, then whatever we are talking about, it is not God.[5]

A problem which has to be addressed is the sense in which God can ever be the stopping point in explanation. To say 'God did it' seems not to end questions, but to create more – why did he make this or that, allow this or that, make people die, allow there to be deserts, make the universe so wretchedly big, create mosquitoes, give life to evil men and women? And to answer those questions, we would need to know the mind of God, and that, religious people say, is a mystery we shall never know.

A point worthy of comment is that in an odd kind of way there is, as Russell and Copleston suggested, a kind of impasse, as if atheist and theist can both agree that either the universe is ultimately explicable, or it is mere brute fact. Either one proposition is true, or the other is; but there seems no obvious way behind that dilemma.

STRETCH AND CHALLENGE

In recent years, there has been interest in the concept of religion without explanation. D. Z. Phillips believed that to seek an explanation was a mistaken enterprise:

Just as there are unquestionable propositions in certain contexts, such as our talk of physical objects, so . . . there are, in one sense, unquestionable beliefs in religion. This is why religion must remain, in a way I try to make clear, without explanation.[6]

He argues that to ask whether God exists is not a theoretical question – if it means anything it is about wonder and praise and prayer. It is life-changing, but as a question which is unanswerable.

From a different perspective, the great Jesuit theologian, Karl Rahner (1904–84) argued:

[Faith is] . . . a letting go of oneself into the incomprehensible mystery. Christianity is far from a clarification of the world and existence; rather it contains the prohibition against treating any experience or insight, however illuminating it may be, as conclusive and intelligible in itself. Christians have [fewer] answers (at their disposal) than other mortals to hand out with a 'now everything is clear'. A Christian cannot enter God as an obvious item in the balance sheet of his life; he can only accept him as an incomprehensible mystery in silence and adoration, as the beginning and end of his hope and therefore as his unique, ultimate and all-embracing salvation.[7]

Exercises and Examination Advice

One way of working on the material in this chapter would be to work with a friend or group of friends and study the two sides of the Copleston–Russell debate. Each of you could learn one side of the debate and then role-play the result and see if either side thinks itself to be winning. This should help you to focus on the strengths and weaknesses of each side of the debate. Then you could try the following:

a. **Explain Copleston's development of the cosmological argument. [25]**

b. **'The world needs no explanation.' Discuss. [10]**

Notes

1. William Temple (1917) *Christus Veritas* (London: Macmillan), p. 7.
2. William Temple (1934) *Nature, Man and God* (London: Macmillan), pp. 131–2.
3. One of the places the debate can be found is http://www.bringyou.to/apologetics/p20.htm. The audio file can be found at http://www.archive.org/details/DebateOnTheExistenceOf GodBertrandRussellV.Fr.FrederickCopleston.
4. Herbert McCabe, O.P. (2000) *God Matters* (London: Mowbray), p. 5.
5. *Ibid* pp.5–6.
6. D. Z. Phillips (1976) *Religion Without Explanation* (Oxford: Blackwell), p. 10.
7. Karl Rahner, S.J. (1979) *Theological Investigations* (London: Darton, Longman & Todd), Vol. 16, pp. 14–15.

The Teleological (Design) Argument

Introduction

The design argument, which in some circles remains a popular argument (for more extended information on Intelligent Design, see Chapter 13) remains, for many, the most successful argument for the existence of God. On the other hand, it is strongly disliked by other religious philosophers, often on the theological ground that it trivializes God – to see him simply as great Designer is held to be anthropomorphizing him, treating him simply as a kind of Superman, but, really, just a better type of architect than his human equivalents.

The argument has been perhaps most prominent during particular times in intellectual history, with its heyday during the late eighteenth and early nineteenth centuries. Many philosophers and theologians were interested in Natural Theology – a whole series of eight books by distinguished scientists and doctors, known as the *Bridgewater Treatises*, endowed by the eccentric Earl, an Anglican cleric who lived in Paris, with his pets fed by liveried waiters off silver plates, was published between 1833 and 1840. Charles Babbage contributed a ninth volume of his own, in 1838. But, by the beginning of the twentieth century, these seemed old-fashioned books. The *Catholic Encyclopaedia* of 1907 argued that this approach had little value as it was based on analogies between particular pieces of nature, such as the hand, and the universe as a whole.

The reason why arguments of this kind had been so popular can be related to the intellectual phenomenon known to us as the Enlightenment, a period which had its roots in the seventeenth century and whose effects are still very much felt today. This movement's origins owe most to the genius of Isaac Newton (1642–1727). We remember him for Newtonian physics, and, in particular, for discovering gravity, but his influence was wider than that. In *Philosophiae Naturalis Principia Mathematica* (1687), Newton, using mathematics and Euclidean geometry, demonstrated how the universe follows mathematical principles – Newton claimed to demonstrate 'the system of the world'.

The intellectual effect of this was colossal – suddenly it appeared as if all the universe was in principle knowable to human reason. In Alexander Pope's famous epitaph:

Nature and Nature's laws lay hid in night;
God said, 'Let Newton be!' and all was light.

Newton had appeared to have demonstrated that the universe ran according to a few simple rules, rather like a machine, and, like a machine, it seemed predictable. It is unsurprising that others sought equally simple solutions to other problems. An obvious example would be Jeremy Bentham, who sought the answer to the mysteries of human behaviour in our egoistic pleasure-seeking and sought a simple, one-principle answer to every problem of living. But we find a similar approach in Kant's attempt to reduce ethical duty to a simple principle of duty, enshrined in the Categorical Imperative, or, a little later, in Karl Marx's attempt to explain all human behaviour and history in terms of simple rules of economics.

Religiously, if the world is a machine, it is straightforward to treat it as requiring a machine-maker. After all, machines are created and engineered – they are not found in nature. In eighteenth-century terms, this model had appeal to deists, who argued that God made the universe and then left it to do its own thing, but, more importantly for us, the model created a pattern of thinking about the universe. If we habitually see it as a machine, if that is the common model for our thought, then it shapes the way we think about it and its creation.

For this reason, as other theories suggested the universe is more complex than that, design arguments became less appealing. Especially significant would be challenges from evolution, but also the Einsteinian and Quantum revolutions in physics would challenge the certainties of Newton. No longer would scientists speak with confidence of the laws of nature – in the twentieth century they spoke rather of theories and principles: Heisenberg's Uncertainty Principle, the Theory of Relativity, Quantum Theory and so on. Karl Popper insisted that science is a set of hypotheses, tested to destruction and replaced by new theories.

Aquinas' Teleological Theory

St Thomas Aquinas' version of the argument is briefly given as the Fifth of his Five Ways. It seems to have been the least significant of his arguments – he deals with it briefly, and hardly returns to it. He writes:

> The fifth way is taken from the governance of the world. We see that things which lack knowledge, such as natural objects, act for a purpose, and this is evident from their acting always – or nearly always – in the same way, to obtain the best result. It is plain that they achieve their end by design and not by chance. It is obvious that something without intelligence could not move towards an end so unerringly unless it were directed by a being with knowledge and intelligence, just as an [inanimate] arrow is directed by an archer. Therefore, some intelligent being exists which directs all natural things to their end. This being we call God.

Notice here that his argument is concerned with design *for a purpose* – things are fitted together to serve a function. Here we see directly the influence of Aristotle's notion that nature is teleological, where everything serves a purpose.

The obvious question is whether that is actually true. If we argue that when we fall into a bed of nettles, we find growing nearby a clump of dock-leaves, the antidote to the stings, it does not answer why the nettles existed in the first place. There is a giveaway in that interpolated 'or nearly always'. If God is all-powerful, then surely there should be no exceptions. Aquinas does not develop what might not work for the best purpose – the mosquito, perhaps? – but it creates a huge gap and a host of questions. We would hardly think our cars well-made if there were bits that were not there for the best functioning of the car. A question also arises that if there are parts of the world that serve no purpose, then from where did they come, if God is supposed to be maker of all things?

Paley's Watch

One version of the argument from design is known as Paley's Watch, which was an analogy used in William Paley's wonderfully titled *Natural Theology: or Evidences of the Existence and Attributes of the Deity Collected from the Appearances of Nature,* which was published in 1802, and which, unsurprisingly, is usually referred to as *Natural Theology*. Paley (1743–1805) was born in Peterborough and studied in Cambridge, where he lectured in moral philosophy, divinity and Greek New Testament. He then held several significant posts in the Church of England, eventually becoming Archdeacon of Carlisle.

Paley's book draws on the science of his day – he notes the complexity of the human brain where millions of cells coordinate together. The human eye is a device of extraordinary flexibility and ability. The wing of a bird and the fin of a fish are wonderfully engineered to allow flight or movement through water. The planets rotate, the seasons advance and recede, with wonderful order. All of this regularity surely points to design, and hence, to a designer.

This point is illustrated by his famous analogy. Suppose I were walking in a wilderness and I came upon a rock lying on the ground. I could account for its existence easily, by reference to natural causes such as wind, erosion, volcanic activity, etc. But suppose instead I came upon a watch; I could not account for it that way. A watch – we are thinking of watches of the pre-digital era – is a wonderful array of intricate cogs, levers, springs, etc. Such a design could not have come about by chance – something must have made it to fit together. There must be a watchmaker.

Paley adds three vital comments:

1. Our inference would not be weaker even if we had never seen a watch before (just as we have not seen God or a world different from this) – the watch is so obviously different from the rock that it must have a different type of source.
2. Even if the watch did not work perfectly – just as the world seems to function imperfectly – there is enough design to enable us to deduce the watchmaker.
3. In the same way, our inference would still hold even if there were parts of the machine whose function we could not work out.

Objections to William Paley

Hume

Perhaps the most cogent arguments against the type of argument offered by Paley can be found in David Hume's *Dialogues Concerning Natural Religion*, published posthumously in 1779. Notice that Hume was not responding to Paley, as this was more than twenty years before the appearance of *Natural Theology*. Nevertheless, his objections are fully applicable to arguments of this type. Hume makes three key objections:

1. **Aptness of Analogy:** As we have suggested, the model used by Enlightenment thinkers, of a machine-like universe, tended to shape their arguments. Hume's argument is similar – what we choose to say the world is like shapes the outcome of the argument. A watch is a machine, and machines have machine-makers. But, consider a cabbage. If we examine its leaves, they are wonderfully fitted together and they serve a purpose as a very healthful form of food. But, if we found a cabbage, we could not go from that to draw the inference that there exists a cabbage-maker. Cabbages we know as natural things, like dandelions or nettles. Is the world any more like a watch than it is like a cabbage or a giant slug or a dandelion? By choosing a machine as our analogy, we have already determined the outcome we want.

2. **The Epicurean Thesis:** Any world is bound to fit together up to a point in order to continue – any significant existence requires a degree of stability and mutual adaptation. The question arises whether such a stable order could randomly arise. Hume suggests one way by reference to the ancient Epicurean Thesis (Nietzsche would revive this theory in *Also Sprach Zarathustra*). Suppose we have infinite time. In infinite time there exists a huge but finite number of particles, freely moving around. In infinite time, these particles would undergo every possible combination. If any one combination happened to represent a stable order, then it must occur. It could be in such a stable order we now live – it is the essence of a stable order that things fit together. (An easy way to remember this argument is to think of the old tale of monkeys in a room full of typewriters. In infinite time, they will type every possible combination of letters, including the Bible, the works of Shakespeare and – indeed – this book.)

3. **Argument from Effect to Cause:** We cannot go from an effect to a cause greater than that needed to produce the cause. Hume gives the example of a set of scales. Suppose we can see only one pan, which, let us say, has a known weight in it. The pan is in the air, so we know that what is in the other pan is heavier. We have no idea whether it is heavier by an ounce or by a ton, and we have no idea whether it is a ton of feathers or an elephant holding it down with his big toe. Equally, the most we could infer from the existence of a watch is that there *was* a watchmaker. We do not and cannot know whether he is still active or even still alive. We cannot say whether he made the watch alone or had some little helpers. In the same way, we cannot go from the facts of this world, with all its limitations, to the infinite, all-loving, all-powerful, all-knowing God in whom most believers wish to place their faith. Hume suggests that perhaps this world is the discarded effort of an infant deity or the work of a committee of gods – we simply cannot know.

Mill

John Stuart Mill (1806–73) pointed to the amount of evil in the world as a fundamental objection to design. He argues:

> Not even on the most distorted and contracted theory of good which was ever framed by religious or
> philosophical fanaticism, can the government of nature be made to resemble the work of a being at
> once good and omnipotent.

His criticism is tied to the problem of evil, but is directed to the idea that, from a
flawed universe, the most we can infer is a flawed creator. There is real evil, not merely
the result of people's free choices (known as *moral* evil) but also, and more significantly, *natural* evil, that is, deaths from illness, plague, volcanoes, earthquakes, fog at
sea, and so on, which seem part of the structure of the world. If these were designed, it
seems a very faulty sort of design, and suggests a designer whose motives we may
doubt. Anthony Kenny has said that this type of argument 'leads to a God which is
no more the source of good than the source of evil. The God to which this argument
of rational theology leads is not supreme goodness: it is a being which is beyond good
and evil'[1]

Darwin

Charles Darwin (1809–82) did not directly attack the Design argument. His own
agnosticism came largely as a result of his encounters with other religions, each claiming to be true, during his world travel on HMS *Beagle*. Indeed, in his most famous
book, *On the Origin of Species by Means of Natural Selection, or The Preservation of
Favoured Races in the Struggle for Life*, usually known as *The Origin of Species* (1859),
he spoke of the way that his theory further pointed to the greatness of God.

But his book raised important questions, if not about the existence of God, then
certainly about traditional easy claims about the nature of the universe as enshrined in
many versions of the Design argument. The earlier work of geologists, many of whom
were clergymen, had already threatened the views of those Christians who wanted to
treat the Genesis account of a seven-day creation literally. Of course, not all Christians
took this literal view of Scripture, neither was it central to faith. In the third century,
Origen, one of the Fathers of the Church, had written:

> For who that has understanding will suppose that the first, and second, and third day, and the
> evening and the morning, existed without a sun, and moon, and stars? And who is so foolish as to
> suppose that first day was, as it were, also without a sky? And who is so foolish as to suppose that
> God, after the manner of a husbandman, planted a paradise in Eden, towards the East, and placed in
> it a tree of life, visible and palpable, so that one tasting of the fruit of tree with the bodily teeth
> obtained life? And again, that one was a partaker of good and evil by masticating what was taken

from the tree? And if God is said to walk in the paradise in the evening, and Adam to hide himself under a tree, I do not suppose that anyone doubts that these things figuratively indicate certain mysteries.

Some, of course, wanted to maintain a literalist account. Philip Gosse (1810–88), a geologist and strict Christian, published, in 1857, *Omphalos*, which claimed, against geologists such as Charles Lyell, that God had comparatively lately made the world in seven days, as the Bible said, but had put in the many geological layers and the fossils as a test of faith.

Darwin's concern was different, arguing not about geology but the development of species. Evolution supports the geological claims in that, like geology, it requires vast stretches of time, and not the creation on Sunday 23 October 4004 BC, suggested by Archbishop Ussher (1581–1656). Species were not fixed on the day of creation, if there had been such a plan. Species had developed blindly and, by what would later be called 'survival of the fittest', either thrived and adapted, or died out – survival of the fittest does not suggest that everything fits together because it is designed that way. We see instead an immensely wasteful process in which species come to exist, but those that do not fit, do not survive. Not all creatures are well adapted to fit in. Nature does not appear to be planned, but haphazard. It does not follow a pattern laid down in advance, or fulfil a purpose – it seems blind. If there is no plan, then surely there is no design.

Other Views and Criticisms

F. R. Tennant in *Philosophical Theology* (1930) suggested a view which has become known as the Anthropic Principle. This argues that the world is so precisely balanced to produce the environment for man that it must surely have been planned. Had earth been closer to or further from the sun, had the elements been different, had things not been just so, then our lives would not have been possible. The chances of our lives occurring in such a well-adapted world are so infinitely small that it must have been planned.

Against this, consider the vast, unimaginably vast, spaces of the universe. The earth is a tiny speck. In most of the universe, as one thinker said, 'nothing very interesting ever happens, and nothing very interesting ever will'. In such a space, with so many variables, the chances that somewhere something happens are much improved. Tennant's view seems to assume that all the vast universe exists for the sake of this little Earth – which seems improbable.

A more modern version is suggested by Richard Swinburne, who concentrates not on the complexity but the simplicity of the universe. He argues that the same hundred or so elements can be combined in so many productive ways, each following the same sets of relatively simple physical laws, that the simplest and most economical explanation would be that God planned it. William of Ockham, in the fourteenth century, had developed the notion that when we have two or more competing theories, the one with the fewer or fewest hypotheses is the most likely to be true. In simple terms, this notion, known as *Ockham's Razor*, is taken to mean that the simplest explanation is the most probable. At the heart of Swinburne's argument is an appeal to this principle. Note, however, that because the simplest explanation is the most likely to be correct, it does not follow that it is correct. In any case, that raises the questions we saw when studying the Cosmological Argument, about whether God really is a simple explanation at all. Indeed, can we even assert that God is the explanation when we cannot say with any precision what type of explanation God might be, given his difference from any type of explanation in our experience?

Exercises and Examination Advice

Make a list of the following terms in your notes and make sure you research them until you have a clear understanding of what each means:

Teleological Argument

Design

Order

Purpose

Evolution

Chaos

It is also important that you make good summary notes on the relevant writings of the following philosophers and thinkers:

Aquinas

Paley

Hume

Mill

Darwin

This is again one of the chapters where, when it comes to examinations, you need to be very clear about what various philosophers have said. It leaves examiners with a poor impression of a response when they read how Hume used evolutionary theory to criticize the design argument or how Mill talked about nature versus machines in his account. These are fairly straightforward critiques of

Aquinas and Paley and a little effort will take your answer from a C grade (knows generally what is said) to a good grade by knowing who said what and, just as importantly, why.

Also keep in mind that understanding and evaluative skills cannot be demonstrated simply by remembering and applying quotations. It is always better to use your knowledge critically. So, for example, 'Mill's use of the problem of evil, where he says ".........." completely undermines the argument from design because . . .' or 'Mill presents no real challenge to the design argument when he says ".........." because . . .' You can apply your quotations here in a thoughtful and critical manner, demonstrating your evaluative skills, rather than stating a quotation and hoping the examiner will read your meaning into it.

With this in mind, try the following:

a. Explain what Paley meant when he described the world as designed. [25]

b. 'Darwin completely undermined Paley's argument.' Discuss. [10]

Note

1. Anthony Kenny (2004) *The Unknown God* (London: Continuum), p. 100.

The Moral Argument 9

Introduction

In many ways, the title '*The* Moral Argument' is misleading. As an argument it takes many forms. You will be examined on Kant's version of the argument. In important respects this is very different from other versions and you must be careful not to attribute to Kant the views of others.

The major forms of the argument, apart from that of Kant, follow one or another of the following forms.

- The benchmark version. This argues that there would be no good without God, that it is God who the basis of standards. The view of St Thomas Aquinas largely follows this pattern.
- The awareness version. This says that our sense of right and wrong is given to us by God and there is no other possible source. John Henry Newman (Cardinal Newman, 1801–90) treated conscience as the voice of God, but did not develop this into a full argument for the existence of God. However, at the popular level, people will sometimes argue that without God, there would be no moral sense. Arguments from Freud and others suggest that the moral sense may have other origins.

Kant's view involves neither of these.

Aquinas' Fourth Way

St Thomas's version of the moral argument is perhaps the least convincing of his Five Ways and can be fairly easily rejected. In his words:

> The fourth way is from the gradation we find in things. Among beings, there are some more or less good, or true, or noble, etc. But 'more' and 'less' are predicated of different things as they more or less, in different ways, resemble a maximum, just as a thing is said to be 'hotter' the more closely it resembles that which is hottest. So it is that there is something which is truest, something best, something noblest, and consequently something that is most real, because those things greatest in truth are greatest in being, as is mentioned in *Metaph*. II. As that book tells us, the maximum in any genus is the cause of all in that genus: fire, the maximum form of heat, causes all hot things. So there must be something which is for everything the cause of its being, its goodness, and every other kind of perfection. We call this being God.

Aquinas is arguing that we determine whether something is better or worse by comparison with the best and greatest in the series. Without that, we could not make the comparison. His justification of this is the assumption from Aristotle's *Metaphysics* that there is a correlation between greatest truth and greatest being. It is difficult to accept this, as truth and being are different types of questions which do not obviously entail each other. For example, '2 + 2 = 4' is necessarily true by the rules of decimal arithmetic, but whether '2' and '4' have being in any sense is a wholly different type of question, of another category. Philosophers sometimes use the term 'category error' for this type of mistaken reasoning.

But there is a simpler way to reject the argument, which is to say that Aquinas is simply wrong to say there has to be a maximum for there to be a comparison of two things. Suppose I have two pens. I can say that this pen writes better than the other, just as I can say that this pen is heavier or longer than that one. To make a comparison I do not need, either mentally or actually, a best of all possible pens (even if such an idea were coherent). I need only two of a series to compare between them.

God as the Source of our Moral Sense

This can, at least some of the time, be related to the common view that morality and the moral sense comes from God. If this view were correct, it would create some special problems of and for faith. In Greece, Plato, in what has become known as the *Euthyphro Dilemma*, questions whether something is right because God commands it, or whether God commands it because it is right.

If we take the view that the sole right-making feature is God's command, and nothing else, we are faced with a serious problem. Some believers will argue, at least initially, that something is right just because God says so (this view is known as Divine Command Theory or Theological Voluntarism), whether in the Ten Commandments, or the Bible, or the Holy Koran or some other source. But a moment's reflection demonstrates the problem. Suppose I were to say to that person, 'Fine, so if God were tomorrow to command me to commit rape, pillage, incest, sheep-worrying, or whatever, these would be the right thing to do?' If the believer says, 'Yes, they would be right,' then clearly she accepts the Divine Command Theory – God's command makes those actions absolutely right. But if she were to say, 'God wouldn't do that,' which, I suggest, is the most likely response, then she would be saying that there is something wrong about these things in themselves – God would not command them because they are wrong.

It could be argued quite plausibly that there are perfectly good human reasons for avoiding certain actions. A world where terrible things are thought perfectly fine would be a vile place in which to live, and most of us prefer not to live in a vile world. Incest, for example, is demonstrably not good for people either physically or emotionally and contributes nothing to human well-being. Most of us find the thought of being murdered undesirable in itself. Rightness and wrongness in these circumstances would seem to be almost matters of fact. Natural Law theorists speak of 'right reason in accordance with nature', arguing that by reasoning along the grain of nature we can see what – at least in general terms – it is right and proper to do. Many of the greatest Natural Law thinkers have been believers, such as Aquinas, but there is no reason why it has to be so. As Hugo Grotius (1583–1645), one of the most distinguished thinkers in this tradition, wrote:

> What we have been saying would have a degree of validity even if we should concede that which cannot be conceded without the utmost wickedness, that there is no God, or that the affairs of men are of no concern to Him.[1]

We can rationally determine what is needed for human flourishing, we want to achieve it, and the moral sense is its achievement. If good is, as some argue, always personal (can there be a good if it is not experienced by a conscious mind?), then the good for persons is simply something that everyone seeks.

Bioethicists such as Edmund O. Wilson and Peter Singer argue that there are sound evolutionary reasons for our ethical sense. Concern for others makes evolutionary sense in terms of the survival of the human species. Singer gives the example of a primitive tribe threatened by sabre-toothed tigers. Suppose the tiger to be faster than the hunters, who hunt in pairs. Mere selfish instinct would tell you to run away, but the tiger is faster and always catches the slower runner. If the two stand and fight for each other, they stand a good chance of beating off the tiger. Sometimes both will die. But by looking out for each other, they reduce the chances of 50 per cent of the hunters being killed and the tribe weakened. Behaviour of this altruistic type is found in animals, where a gazelle might distract a lion at the cost of its own life so the herd as a whole is saved.

The theological complication is that if God is simply the law-giver, then he becomes less than the good God in whom worshippers believe. 'I'm right because I say so' is an unconvincing argument when uttered by parents, and no less unconvincing as a sign of goodness. It would also leave little space for human ethical behaviour beyond blind obedience, and would cause problems for the Free Will defence in the problem of evil.

Much religious thought emphasizes the need for separation of morality from faith, not least to explain how those with no knowledge of the Christian faith could nevertheless hold many, perhaps most, ethical teachings in common. This is important to the Natural Law tradition, as suggested. William Temple said, 'In its nature, the moral judgment is quite wholly independent of religion.'

Freud and Psychological Views

Sigmund Freud (1856–1939) provides an alternative, naturalistic, account of how moral responsibility and guilt feelings could occur. For Freud, conscience was essentially the internalizing of parental prohibitions and demands, so they seem to come from within ourselves. This creates an aspect of our minds known as the *superego*.

For Freud, there are three parts of what he calls the psychic apparatus – the *id*, which is our instincts, unorganized and a bit chaotic; the *ego*, which is the organized and more realistic part of the mind; and the *superego*, which criticizes the rest and is the moralizing function. (Incidentally, the terms used here were not part of Freud's vocabulary, but were used by the translator into English. Freud could be more accurately translated as 'the It', 'the I' and the 'Over-I'. Had the translator used Freud's terms, connections with some other aspects of German thought would have been much more clear.) For Freud, the newborn child is all *id*, with basic drives such as those for food, aggression and sex. This part of the mind is amoral, egocentric, pleasure-seeking. On the other hand, the *ego* is rational, capable of controlling the *id*. Freud gives the analogy of a horse and rider. The rider (*ego*) controls the way the horse (*id*) goes. Sometimes, control fails and the horse goes the way it wishes to go, over rocky terrain.

But the *ego* has to battle with the external world and the *superego* as well as with the *id*. When this happens, the *ego* tends to be more loyal to the *id*, avoiding conflict, excusing problems. The *superego*, however, watches the *ego*'s actions like a hawk, punishing it with feelings of inferiority, anxiety and general guilt. The *ego* does have defence mechanisms, such as fantasy, rationalization, repression and others.

For Freud, the *superego* symbolically internalizes the sense of a father figure and the regulations found in society. It tends to oppose the *id*, giving us a sense of the moral and setting up taboos against certain types of feelings and actions. If the Oedipus Complex (which inclines men to sleep with their mothers and kill their fathers) is particularly repressed, through parents, schooling and authority figures in general, the stricter will be the rule of the *superego* over the *ego*, and the stronger the sense of the moral and of conscience castigating our urges.

The scientific basis of these theories is disputed by many psychologists, scientists and philosophers. Freud himself tended to construct theories on relatively little empirical evidence, and it is not easy to see how some of these might be tested. Karl Popper argued that much psychology was not scientific as it involved hypotheses which were not falsifiable – that is, it was not possible to say precisely what would prove them incorrect. According to Popper, real science is always falsifiable. If we say that pure water always boils at 100° Celsius, we can see precisely what would falsify it – an instance of pure water boiling at a different temperature. But it is difficult to see what would falsify the claim that the *superego* acts in the way that Freud suggests.

Indeed, the Oedipus Complex itself is strongly disputed. Freud based it on a belief that he drew from *The Golden Bough* by Sir James Frazer (1854–1941). In its time, this was an immensely influential work on anthropology and religion. It was first published in two volumes, in 1890; by its third edition (1906–15) it had stretched to twelve. Wittgenstein was fascinated by it, and often discussed it. Much of it has been subsequently discredited or ignored, but it still contains valuable insights. Freud drew on the theory of the Primal Horde.

Once, in primitive times, the theory says, there was the Primal Horde, a tribal group dominated by the Old Man. He was stronger and more cunning than any of the other males, and exercised total rights over the females. The young men disputed this, but if anyone challenged him, he would be beaten off. In the end, the young men got together, ambushed the Old Man, killed him, ate him (they were cannibals) and started to have their way with the women. But disputes broke out over the women. Gradually the young men started to think there had been a point in some of the Old Man's rules and began to feel regret at his death.[2] From that we get our taboo against incest, and in their collective guilt is the origin of the guilt we feel, passed down through the collective unconscious.

Needless to say, there is not a shred of evidence for this deeply moving tale, which might form the basis of a box office hit at the cinema. But it was on that basis that Freud constructed his notion of the Oedipus Complex.

Whatever the faults of Freud, he provided a theory which explained the moral sense in terms other than that God gave it to us. We could readily construct a more plausible argument by pointing to the notion that we get our sense of guilt and responsibility from our upbringing or authority figures. There is little doubt that our early experiences shape our world picture, even if there is argument over precisely how this shaping takes place. Above all, Freud should shake any belief that God is our only explanation for the moral sense.

Kant and the Moral Argument

Kant's version of the argument is wholly different from any others we have seen. For Kant, there are three postulates of practical reason – that we are immortal, that God exists, and that we are free beings. For Kant, a key value is *autonomy*, that is, the notion that we are wholly free beings. We are capable of choice and, above all, are rational beings.

This freedom of choice entails the ability to determine what is right and wrong, which Kant does through the notion of the Categorical Imperative, which works out the implications of the rational awareness that we should always do our duty without regard for the consequences. We ought, rationally, to do our duty for its own sake.

The thing to notice here is that we do our duty *because* it is rational to do so, and not because God has commanded it. If we did what was right because God commanded it, or had ethical rules laid down by God, or our reason had been determined by God, we would not be autonomous creatures, but heteronomous, that is, directed by another.

Remember that for Kant, the existence of God is a postulate of practical reason. We cannot prove by conventional metaphysics the existence of God, because he lies outside any possible experience, and we have seen Kant's rejection of Ontological Arguments. To be a postulate means that the point is taken for granted.

The argument Kant does give can be summarized easily:

- Rationally, perfect virtue ought to be rewarded by perfect happiness;
- The combination of perfect happiness and perfect goodness is the *summum bonum* ('highest good');
- Clearly this is not achieved in this life. Good things happen to bad people and catastrophes to the virtuous;
- Therefore, because the *summum bonum* ought to be achieved, it can be achieved;
- If it is not achievable in this life, it must be achievable in the next;
- If the *summum bonum* exists in the next life, there must be someone to provide it;
- This someone is obviously God.

The argument is not very convincing. Much debate has concentrated on the assumption that *ought* implies *can*. Kant's notion seems to be that if it makes no sense to tell someone that she ought to do something if it is impossible to do so, then whenever we say *ought*, *can* necessarily follows. If I say, 'You ought to be kind to your mother,' it makes sense because it is possible for you to do so, provided you have contact with your mother. If I said, 'You ought to flap your arms and take off,' there can be no sense to *ought* as what I am demanding of you is impossible. But in Kant's moral argument is a different use of *ought* – it is an *ought* of what should exist, not of duty. *Ought* has many meanings. That I ought to be paid more does not entail the implication that my employer has the money to give me the pay rise I so richly deserve. In the same way, that bad things happen to good people does not mean that *therefore* compensation or justice will be forthcoming. If I say that they *ought* to be recompensed, I am expressing a wish, not saying that they will receive justice or even that it is possible they will do so.

A further weakness has been indicated by Brian Davies. If the *summum bonum* does indeed exist, why should it need God to provide it? Remember Hume's objections to Design Arguments. It is possible that the *summum bonum* is the creation of a committee of lesser Gods, an angel or whoever. All that would be needed is a being of sufficient power to achieve the result. We would still be left far short of the God in whom believers wish to believe.

Behind Kant's whole approach seems to be the assumption that the universe is fair. But, why should it be? Life may just be unfair and all we can do is to try to make the best of it. Unless it is possible to demonstrate the intrinsic fairness of things, it seems irrational to assert that they just, in the end, are. Simply wishing it were otherwise does not make it so.

Exercises and Examination Advice

Make a list of the following terms in your notes and make sure you research them until you have a clear understanding of what each means

Moral Argument

Summum Bonum

Inferences

Innate Morality

Id

Ego

Superego

Categorical Imperative

It is also important that you make good summary notes on the relevant writings of the following philosophers and thinkers:

Kant

Freud

A good place to start working on this chapter is to explore what Kant understood by the idea of reason and its importance to him. You could for example explore whether or not you agree that all morality must be reasonable. The idea that once the categorical imperative test has been applied the maxim must be followed, for example, is at least questionable in its more extreme applications. Would you for example really not lie to a serial killer who was searching for your sibling?

You could then explore the debate as to whether or not moral awareness is in fact innate or something learned as we grow up. It is important, though, to keep in mind that the focus of this debate must come back to philosophy, not ethics. Ultimately you will be looking at the question of whether or not this view of morality really leads to a proof of God's existence. You should remember while you are doing this that Kant himself thought that proving God's existence would be a bad thing for our moral behaviour.

Then try:

a. Explain a moral argument for the existence of God. [25]

b. 'Freudian psychology undermines Kant's moral argument.' Discuss. [25]

Notes

1. Hugo Grotius (1625) *De Iure Belli ac Pacis*, Prolegomena, §11.
2. This account can be found in Freud's *Totem and Taboo* (1913), a book which shows Freud at his most speculative.

The Problem of Evil 1 – St Augustine

Introduction

For many, the Problem of Evil is the most intractable of all objections to the existence of God. In people's lives, evil is experienced as a reality in ways that other experiences are not. People are changed by evil. Pain hurts. In our lives, we meet people embittered – understandably – by the pain and anguish they have suffered. Others appear to rise above their pain, not merely facing adversity with cheerfulness, but seeming enriched by the experience. We find it difficult to blame the former, while the latter fill us with admiration.

Evil and pain seem to be interwoven into the very fabric of the world. The twentieth century produced suffering on an industrial scale. Lenin developed the theory of terror as a political tool, and terror became commonplace, whether in the Civil War in Russia, in Stalin's cruelties, Hitler's death camps and murder squads, Mao's China or Pol Pot's Kampuchea. Warfare has developed weapons of mass destruction, terrorists kill indiscriminately, and there are uncounted smaller cruelties. Nor is evil something only fully recognized in modern times – ancient writings give stark testimony to cruelty and anguish. Nature too brings its own sufferings, in epidemics, pandemics, earthquakes, tsunamis, cyclones and pains as real as the mosquito's bite.

It is important to note that evil is always an evil experienced by someone or groups of people. Evil does not present itself as a theoretical problem but as an inescapable reality of living. This suggests that no answer given can be simply theoretical. If evil presents itself as *my* suffering or *your* anguish, then any answer must be addressed to the place where the suffering exists. To the frightened woman standing on the edge of the death-pit with her tiny baby, any answer has to be one that speaks to her. Can any answer be given that is remotely credible?

People sometimes look for a casual response – a particularly thoughtless one is along the lines that we need the black to appreciate the white, the darkness to see the light, or evil to see the good. Such a response is morally inadequate, reducing evil to aesthetics. Essentially, this is a third-person or ideal observer position. An ideal observer outside the world might look down and appreciate a picture, noting the contrasts. But this is not how evil is experienced. It is not a picture seen by a distant observer but something that involves real harm to real people. To say that these Gypsies or Jews were exterminated so that good could grow out of their suffering or so an observer could truly appreciate the good says nothing to those who died.

Is it possible to find any kind of answer to the immensity of human suffering which does not involve God in wilful neglect?

The Problem Defined

The Problem of Evil is traditionally defined in terms of an inconsistent triad. This has been given in various forms by philosophers as varied as Epicurus and David Hume. The key elements are:

1. If God were all-powerful, he would be able to abolish evil.
2. If God were all-loving, then he would wish to abolish evil.
3. But evil exists.

Therefore, God is not all-powerful, or not all-loving, or both.

Notice immediately that this is not an objection to any kind of God. Aristotle's God would be quite indifferent to human suffering. In the same way, one could imagine a couch-potato God who injects pain and anguish into the world to make it more entertaining for himself – he likes horror movies. But the God of Abraham, Isaac and Jacob, the God of Christian faith, is a God who is intimately bound up with his creation, who loves and cares for all those within it.

One line of defence seems to be immediately ruled out. A Christian believer cannot take the path of arguing that evil is not real. (The Church of Christ Scientist, founded by Mary Baker Eddy, does argue for the illusory nature of evil, but it is not considered a Christian Church by other denominations. In any case, if I experience a pain as a pain, even if it is a figment of my imagination, it is nonetheless a pain, experienced as such.) Notice that the Bible presents evil as starkly and brutally real. If the suffering of Christ were merely illusory, his redemptive death would become a fraud. Scripture presents his death in brutally real and absolutely real terms. Some have argued that what Jesus shows is that God does not remove suffering but shows the world that he will never desert humanity in its suffering: indeed, it has been suggested, by Hans Küng among others, that God suffered on the cross so that he could look suffering humanity in the face. This might, theologically, present important religious truth about how God relates to the world, but it deepens the mystery of why God allows the evil in the first place.

There are conventionally taken to be two aspects to the problem – *moral evil*, which is the evil that flows from human choices, raising the question of why God permits humans to behave as they do; and *non-moral evil* or *natural evil* or *suffering*, which is the evil that follows from sources other than human choice, such as hurricanes, earthquakes and much disease. Of course, it is not always possible to see where the division can be made. If I knowingly choose to live in an earthquake zone, or voluntarily indulge in dangerous activities, then there is at least an element of moral evil in any harm that might befall me.

Any attempt to justify the goodness of God in the face of evil is known as a *theodicy*. Of theodicies, perhaps the best known is that of St Augustine.

The Theodicy of St Augustine of Hippo

St Augustine (354–430) was one of the greatest and certainly one of the most influential of all Christian thinkers. In his younger days – well documented in his *Confessions* – he was a Manichaean. The Manichees were especially influential in North Africa, where he lived. Their doctrine was perhaps a perversion of Platonism. For Plato, the material was inferior to the spiritual, but good insofar as it participated in the realm of the Forms. In various heresies, such a view was perverted into the simplification that things spiritual were good, those material were evil. For the Manichaeans, matter and spirit had different origins, coming from different gods. The task of the believer was to liberate the good, which was purely spiritual, from the wickedness of matter. The logical consequence, of course, was suicide, but in practice it was the denial of the material aspects of life. Manichaeanism was perhaps the most extreme of that body of heresies which make up Gnosticism.

That these heresies presented danger to the Christian Church can be seen by reflection on the Nicene Creed, associated with the Council of Nicaea (325). The opening clauses continually repeat the belief in one God, the creator of all that is, whether seen or unseen in heaven or under the earth. In the original ending, any other view is specifically anathematized.

After his Christian conversion, St Augustine stressed that the universe is good, or, at least, that it was made good. In Genesis, God sees that that which he made is good. Therefore, evil is the going wrong of something itself made good. The flavour of Augustine's argument can be seen in the following extract from *Enchiridion* 10–12:

> By the Trinity, which is supremely and equally and unchangeably good, all things were created. These things are not equally, supremely and unchangeably good, but they remain good, even taken separately. Taken together, they are very good, because they make up the universe in all its wonderful order and beauty.
>
> In the universe, even that which we call evil, when it is regulated and put in its own place, only enhances our admiration of the good; for we enjoy and value the good more when we compare it with the evil. For almighty God, who, as even the heathens admit, has supreme power over all things, being Himself supremely good, would never permit the existence of anything evil among what he has made, unless through his omnipotence and goodness that he could create good even from evil. For what is that which we call evil but the absence of good? In the bodies of animals, disease and wounds mean nothing except the absence of health. When a cure is achieved, that does not mean that the evils – namely, the diseases and wounds – go away from the body and live elsewhere. They completely cease to exist; for the wound or disease is not a substance, but a defect in the fleshly substance. The flesh itself is a substance, and therefore something good, of which those evils – that is, privations of that good we call health – are accidents. In exactly the same way, what are called vices in the soul are nothing but privations of natural good.

There is much to notice here. Most obviously, there is an element of the aesthetic argument we rejected earlier, that harm enables us to admire good. More interesting, perhaps, is the notion that everything made is good, but not in the same way as the goodness of God. This means that if God makes that which is not God, he makes it good, but *in its own way*. If we think about this, we can understand what Augustine means. Consider a stone. A stone may be argued to be good, but only in the way a stone can be good – good for building, for skipping over water, in its purity or whatever. A stone can only be good as a stone can be. It cannot be good in the way a horse is good – horses are different in kind from stones and are good in quite different ways. And the goodness of humans is very different from the goodness of stones or horses. A horse cannot be a good author and is not good as a building material. If God makes things in all different ways, then, inevitably, while being good in themselves, there will be a scale of goods. Things will be more or less good in different respects. The very act of creation seems to involve the introduction of beings more or less good in different respects.

Augustine introduces the notion that evil is a privation. We must be careful here – he is not denying the reality of evil. Father Herbert McCabe used to say that nothing in the wrong place is just as real as something in the wrong place. If someone drives his car over a cliff, it is the nothingness beneath his car he has to worry about. In the same way, someone whose mind turns to evil has become a human being gone badly wrong. As a human being, Adolf Hitler was good in himself – the evil came when he became less than a human being.

To explain the evil in the world, itself made good, Augustine looks to two events – the Fall of Angels and the Fall of Man. In the first, certain angels, led by Lucifer, chose to reject God. In their choice – which was not the choice of God – they introduced the evil of denial and fell into hell. Subsequently, Adam and Eve, in the Garden of Eden, chose to reject God's command. For their act of defiance they were punished by expulsion from the place of bliss.

For Augustine, the punishment continues to our own day. All evil, for Augustine, is either the *result* of sin or punishment *for* sin. We are punished because all mankind was seminally present in the loins of Adam. Natural evil flows from the disorder brought into the fabric of the universe by the original sin of our ancestors both human and angelic. God does not cease to love us, despite our sinfulness, and offers the possibility of redemption through the saving work of his son, Jesus.

The Free Will Defence

This theodicy is sometimes described as a *soul-deciding* theodicy. The choice is ours. By our lives we choose whether to obey God or not.

An important part of St Augustine's philosophy was a belief in Will. You will recall from our discussion of Plato that he lacked a word for Will and explained wrongdoing in terms of ignorance of the good. St Augustine believed that we could know the good yet still not do it. We have will – we can choose what we do. This is important to various theodicies. The notion is that we have free choice and that this is central to being truly good.

Imagine a young man falling on his knees before a girl, pouring out a tale of his love for her. He tells her of his undying love, that she is the light of his life, that he wishes nothing more than to be with her. She, slightly taken aback, asks why he loves her so much. He explains that her father has told him he will be shot if he does not take the daughter off his hands. If he does marry her, he will be rewarded by large sums of money. In these circumstances, it would not be too surprising if the girl had some doubts about the love being expressed. In a genuine relationship, there is always the hidden premise that the love has to be freely given if it is to mean anything. In real relationships, the love one has for the other comes daily as a welcome surprise. The love is genuine because it could be otherwise. 'Why me?' is a central question in any true love. Knowing that you are the chosen one is the central mystery of relationship and what, at the same time, gives it its infinite value. In the same way, if we are to have a genuine love for God, it must be freely given. It could be otherwise, on both sides of the relationship. That is why freedom of the will is so important. Augustine argues that a world with the evils that follow from free will is better than one without it:

> The generosity of God's goodness is such that he has not stopped himself from creating that creature which he foreknew would not merely sin but determine to remain sinful. Just as a runaway horse is better than a stone which cannot run away because it lacks self-direction and perception, so the creature which sins by free will is better than the one which does not sin because it has no free will.

J. L. Mackie has questioned this, in his article 'Evil and Omnipotence' (*Mind*, April 1955, p. 209). He argues that some people have free will and yet we know by their character they will always do the right thing – they are reliable even though they could choose otherwise. Mackie asks whether God could not make creatures with free will but, because of their character, guaranteed to do the right thing. This would not be logically impossible. The obvious objection to this is that if God made people guaranteed to do the right thing, they would feel free to themselves, but they would not be free in the relationship that really mattered – the one with God. They would not surprise God by their love.

Objections to St Augustine

There is much that is controversial in this theodicy. The obvious problem is that it depends on a very literal reading of scripture. It treats Genesis as history of actual events. Secondly, his science is flawed. In ancient times, there was a theory of *homunculi*, which believed that a man contained large numbers of little people. In successful intercourse, the little person was planted in the woman's womb. Medical textbooks showed a man's loins populated with little fellows. This view is now rejected – the woman contributes the egg. We do not pre-exist conception. You and I were not present in Eden. And, even if we were, it seems very unfair that we should carry the blame for the actions of someone else. After all, we considered it an advance in humanity when in our legal systems we ceased to punish entire families for the crimes of one of their members.

Philosophically, the question of Augustine is even more complex. If creation were made perfectly, it would not go wrong. It is the inability to go wrong that we would expect from perfection. If God had made hell as a place to send the wicked, then he had built into the universe not only the possibility of imperfection but also a place of torment and suffering. That could hardly be making it good.

Augustine was inconsistent in his use of the free will defence. In Book I of *De Libero Arbitrio* (Of the Freedom of the Will) Augustine develops an idea of the freedom of the will, arguing in Chapter 2 that the responsibility for an action lies with the person who performs it – it is his responsibility, not God's (Book I.11). By Book III Augustine talks of the ignorance of human nature, suggesting even that we cannot overcome our wretched condition (*De Libero Arbitrio* III.18). On this latter reading it is difficult to see how the Free Will Defence is justifiable, as it presupposes the conditions in which we can make genuine and *informed* choices. It seems unjustified to punish people for ignorance which is not their own responsibility as they could do nothing about it. Augustine's views on Predestination, the idea that God knows in advance and determines our eventual fate, also weaken his version of the Free Will Defence. For Augustine, our election to heaven is a matter for the inscrutable will of God. His intention was to oppose the heresy of Pelagianism, which argued that humanity could achieve salvation by its own unaided efforts (according to William Temple, this is 'the only intrinsically damnable heresy') – there had to be a role for God. But, in the response to this, Augustine appears to have undermined his own defence against evil.

Exercises and Examination Advice

Make a list of the following terms in your notes and make sure you research them until you have a clear understanding of what each means:

The Problem of Evil

The theodicy of Augustine

Natural Evil

Moral Evil

Merited Suffering

Unmerited Suffering

The responsibility of God in the existence of evil

The origins of evil

Human Free Will

It is also important that you make good summary notes on the relevant writings of the following philosophers:

Epicurus

David Hume

Augustine

There are many kinds of exercises you could do to learn the material in this chapter. You could, for example, start with the Manichaean background of St Augustine and explore how these ideas can be found throughout history and literature. In fact, working in a group you could each explore different areas. To take a more modern example, you could discuss the use of the idea of two forces controlling the universe in the *Star Wars* films.

Alternatively, you could look at the possible interpretations of merited and unmerited suffering. I find my students often see prisons as a kind of merited suffering, to which I usually add the idea of a hangover; a significant number often empathize with the later idea.

The idea of free will for human beings is another area which has a wide range of possible routes to explore. Those who have studied ethics will be well aware of the concepts of Hard Determinism, Soft Determinism and Compatabilism. Again, though, you will need to be careful that you focus on the philosophy issues here and do not become too tied up with the ethics. The ultimate focus needs to be on whether or not human free will really justifies the extent of evil in the world.

Then try these:

a. **Explain what philosophers mean by theodicies. [25]**

b. **'No theodicy can ever justify the existence of evil.' Discuss. [10]**

The Problem of Evil 2 – Irenaean Theodicy **11**

Introduction

In recent years, and especially since the publication of John Hick's *Evil and the God of Love* (1966), there has been a revival of interest in what is called Irenaean Theodicy.

St Irenaeus was born early in the second century, probably in Smyrna (Izmir) in Turkey, and was probably of Greek origin. He came from a Christian family and was a protégé of Polycarp, who, by tradition, was a member of the circle of St John the Evangelist. Irenaeus spent some time in Rome, but a major part of his life was spent in Lyons (then called Lugdunum), in Gaul (France) as both priest and bishop. He died in about AD 200. His major work, still extant, is *Adversus Haereses* ('Against Heretics'). Fragments of other works are known, and among his lost books is *On the Monarchy, or How God is not the Cause of Evil*.

Throughout his work he is especially concerned with the errors of the Gnostic heresy. In all its forms, the central belief of Gnosticism is that matter is evil. It follows from this that God, if he is good, cannot be responsible for matter. Equally, Jesus, if truly the Son of God, could not have a material body. Against this Irenaeus would hold that everything is from God, something that would be further supported at Nicaea in 325, as we have seen in the last chapter.

But if matter is of God, and not evil, then evil needs another explanation.

The Theodicy of Irenaeus

For Irenaeus himself, the key to understanding evil is to recognize that the evil of the world can serve a purpose. Irenaeus' theodicy is sometimes described as a process of soul-making, as opposed to the 'soul-deciding' theodicy of Augustine.

The key text for this approach is Genesis 1.26. Here God wishes to make man 'in his own image and likeness'. This means that we are made in God's *image* but need to grow, throughout history, into his *likeness*. Irenaeus treats Adam and Eve as children in their moral immaturity. Like children, they disobeyed a simple rule. He does not treat this as a catastrophe – it is part of growing up. He does not have the sense of Original Sin found in later writers. God intended man to mature over a lengthy time, sending Christ as part of that learning process. God sends evil to help us. We learn the right way through experience, in the way that Jonah learnt repentance through his time in the belly of the whale. Without evils like death and other pains we would not learn the need for goodness and repentance. If everything were easy, there would be no virtue – worthwhile things are gained with effort. We need also to learn that we must be patient, to allow God to make his world as he chooses. A favourite image is God as a potter moulding his clay. He says:

> You do not make God: God makes you. As God's workmanship you should wait for the hand of your Maker who makes everything in his time. For yourself, your creation is being carried out. Offer to God your heart in a soft and mouldable state, preserving the form in which the Creator first made you. Keep yourself moist so you do not become too hard for his fingers to work. By keeping this structure, you will rise to perfection, for your moist clay is hidden by God's workmanship. His hand fashioned your being. He will cover you on the inside and outside with purest silver and gold. He will adorn you so well that 'the King himself will take pleasure in your beauty'. But, if you let yourself be hardened, then you reject the work of his skill. Your ingratitude, ignoring his goodness in creating you human, will mean you have lost his work on you, and with this, you will lose your life. (*Against Heresies,* IV.xxxix.2)

The work of God is ongoing, in Christ working with our efforts. What St Irenaeus balances is the free choice of humanity with the working of God as essential to our salvation. He avoids any hint of Pelagianism, which argued that we can be worthy of God wholly through our own efforts, roughly two centuries before that particular heresy arose. On the other hand, his apparent indifference to Original Sin or the theology of the Fall would raise questions for the future.

John Hick's Version

In *Evil and the God of Love* (1966), the distinguished British philosopher of religion John Hick (1922–) developed this theodicy. He takes the basic idea of soul-making, but spells out its implications.

The key to Hick's argument is that something's goodness may depend very much on its purpose. He argues that a world without pain or the possibility of pain might be a very good world in itself, but it would not be a good world for the purpose of soul-making. If God made this to be a world in which we could develop, then this creation suits that purpose very well.

Central to Hick's version is the place of genuine freedom. He accepts the Free Will Defence, arguing that God wants genuine relationship with us. He argues that the only relationship worth having is one which is freely chosen. Its precondition is free choice. But, if we are genuinely to have real choices then real consequences must be possible. If it is impossible for you to be hurt, then I am not free to choose to hurt you. And if everything in your garden is rosy, then nothing I can do will help you, either. If I can become a good person only by performing genuinely good acts, then a good (or harm) must be experienceable. The possibility of real harm and good is essential.

Nor is this simply a matter of freedom of action. It is also essential to freedom of understanding. Suppose no harm can come from any of my actions; then God would need continually to intervene. Sometimes the knife in my hand would be hard and sharp, when I needed it to cut my bread, but soft and blunt if I tried to plunge it into you. To keep this continual change, God would need endlessly to act to alter the world. But if he did, then the only explanation for things would have to be God. There would be no regularity in nature – things would be sometimes soft and sometimes hard. Without the possibility of regularity, there would be no possibility of science. Science depends for its theories on finding regularity in things. But if there were no science, there would be no explanation except God for anything. We could find no other possibility. We would be forced to recognize God, and so would have no choice in our relationship with him. To retain that relationship, we need the possibility of other explanations. So Hick says that God creates an *Epistemic Distance*, a gap in knowledge, that permits us to come to our own conclusions.

What Hick says about Natural Evil is implicit in the account already given. He develops a counter-factual thesis, asking what the world would be like if it were not like this, if there were no pain. The world, he argues, would be rather like that portrayed in Tennyson's *The Lotos-Eaters*, a meaningless, empty haze. Real courage, patience, charity – virtues which enable people to become more worthwhile, to be more themselves – would be impossible. Many ordinary activities would become impossible. A cricket match in which the ball was hard to be hit, but soft when caught, where the bowler never suffered the anguish of failing to take a wicket, nor the batsman the indignity of being out or failing to reach the boundary, would be an impossibility. Fair play and application would be meaningless. Human life and interest would be lost. More significantly, none of us would grow into the likeness of God.

So far, Hick has simply developed Irenaeus. In one important area, he takes a direction that is directly opposed to the earlier view. Hick believes in universal salvation. Irenaeus himself suggests the continuation of soul-making into the next life. But he is in no doubt that those who reject God are damned. He says:

> It is one and the same God who prepared good things with himself for those who seek his fellowship and obey him, and who has created eternal fire for the devil, the leader of apostasy and those who fell with him. Into this fire he will send those men who are on his left hand, having set themselves apart. . . . [He makes] peace and friendship with those who return to him, bringing unity, but prepares for those who reject the light, impenitent, eternal fire and outer darkness, which are truly evils for those who fall into them. (*Against Heresies*, IV, xI, 1)

For Hick, hell is part of the problem of evil. If the whole purpose of evil is to produce good, then, argues Hick, we cannot explain hell. It does no good except to cause pain and punishment. Therefore, Hick takes a view of hell which is essentially purgatorial. Roman Catholics believe that on death, those who have chosen God, but are not yet worthy to be with him, go to a place of purgation, where they undergo further preparation for their eternal glory with God. Such is Hick's view of Hell – a place of temporary suffering.

This view has its own problems. The place of further soul-making has much to appeal. Even the great villains, provided they eventually repent and purge their evils, are not outside the love of God. But, if the whole purpose of soul-making is to permit us the freedom to choose or reject God, then if we spend all eternity with God, regardless, the point of free will seems difficult to discern. We might attempt to claim that hell is our voluntary separation from God, painful though that is, rather than a place of fire and torture (Aquinas takes this view), but there is still endless pain, without hope of improvement. Some might make the case, known as annihilationism, that if we reject God, we are not rewarded with eternal life. There is nothing. We do not suffer, but simply cease to be.

Hick remains very aware that his theodicy might seem too glib. He is aware that he can at best justify suffering in general. There is a weight of suffering on earth that seems to serve no purpose – he speaks of pains where

> . . . we can see no gain to the soul, whether of the victim or others, but on the contrary only a ruthlessly destructive purpose which is utterly inimical to human values. . . . Instead of ennobling, affliction may crush the character and wrest from it whatever virtues it possessed.[1]

This evil – called dysteleological evil – remains a problem. Hick hopes for a future so great and good that it justifies even the greatest pain. But he does not underrate the difficulty with his view.

STRETCH AND CHALLENGE

One of the most controversial modern theodicies is that of Richard Swinburne. Its basic premise is that natural or physical evil is a precondition of moral evil, a view different from the traditional idea of St Augustine that natural evil is a consequence of, or punishment for, sin. Swinburne argues that the existence of many natural evils is logically necessary for agents to have *knowledge* of how to bring about evil or prevent it. They need this knowledge if they are to have a genuine choice between bringing about evil and bringing about good.

There are seven stages to the argument which supports this view:

1. Agents gain knowledge inductively from present events about what will happen in the future.
2. If agents are knowingly to bring about or prevent certain circumstances, they must know that consequences follow from their actions.
3. Agents can only know that certain actions will have bad consequences if they have prior knowledge of those consequences.
4. We can only know these bad consequences if others have suffered them before (I have no prior experience of my own death).
5. For any evil act (such as murder), there must have been a first instance. The perpetrator of the first murder cannot have known the consequences of his action from seeing someone else murdered.
6. Therefore, the first perpetrator must have gained his knowledge from having seen or heard of this action having dire consequences (e.g. a rock falling on someone's head and killing him).
7. There must be many natural evils for us to know the range of possible evils, and many instances of these to give us sufficient inductive knowledge.

Swinburne argues forcibly that only by providing this wide range does God provide the opportunity to exercise responsibility. Only by allowing great horrors can he give us the gift of full freedom. Against the view that the sheer scale of the horror of Auschwitz or Hiroshima is simply too great to justify God, Swinburne says:

> What in effect the objection is asking is that a God should make a toy-world, a world where things matter, but not very much; where we can choose and our choices can make a small difference, but the real choices remain God's. For he simply would not allow us the choice of doing real harm, or through our negligence allowing real harm to occur. He would be like the over-protective parent who will not let his child out of sight for a moment.

At a theological level, there are several objections to Swinburne's argument:

- God's purpose is seen as primarily didactic: he is presented primarily as a teacher of moral truths, providing unlimited lessons in the possibility of evil. A Christian might ask, where in all this is he to find the God of love and justice? A parent content to let his child play on the railway line to learn this is dangerous is not to be defended by saying he does not want to be over-protective – he is culpably morally negligent.

- We might properly ask whether this theodicy provides the answer which has to be given to the victim. Any satisfactory answer has to be directed to the one who suffers. Suffering is not an intellectual puzzle which makes sense to an ideal observer: if it is to be answered, it has to be answered at the level of the victim, for suffering is always something experienced by a person. In Swinburne's world picture, the victim has suffered the evil that others might learn their responsibilities. Much attention has been paid to Swinburne's frequent assertion that those who suffer know that they have been of use to others as a lesson to others – that the worst thing of all would be not to have been of use. This has seemed to critics both coldly utilitarian and little answer to the Auschwitz prisoner herded into the gas-chamber with her child as one among countless victims. The horror would not have been mitigated or the lesson any less if that one mother and child had been spared.
- We might ask where is the justice if, at the end of things, people still have not learned and still perpetrate great evils.
- We should note that Swinburne does not attempt to answer the question which John Hick asks about his own Irenaean theodicy:

> . . . if we ask whether the business of soul making is worth all the toil and sorrow of human life, the Christian answer must be in terms of a future good great enough to justify all that has happened on the way to it.[2]

Swinburne does consider the view that God will use an afterlife to compensate people for the pains they have suffered in life. He says that he sees strong reasons to hold to this hypothesis, but says that adding it to his already complex theistic hypothesis, based on a Bayesian theory of probability, would diminish the prior probability on which that idea depends.

A philosopher might object to Swinburne's theodicy by using Popper's argument that we do not learn inductively, but by the hypothetico-deductive method. This presupposes that we are capable of developing theories on very few observations. Swinburne bases his whole argument on the assumption that learning is inductive. Even if he were correct, he appears to underestimate the capacity of the human brain to extrapolate from experience. I do not need to see a living skull crushed to work out the fragility of human life. I might learn that crushing pods on plants or breaking eggs has certain effects: I might then hypothesize that cracking someone's skull might have similar effects. The point is learnable without a deity ensuring that rocks fall on someone's head to act as a lesson for the survivors on how to kill each other.

Objections to Soul-making Theodicy

In 2004, D. Z. Phillips (1934–2006) published *The Problem of Evil and the Problem of God*, bringing together many of his earlier ideas, challenging many assumptions of twentieth-century theodicy, in particular the efforts of Hick and Swinburne.

The distinctive feature of Phillips' general philosophical approach is a lively awareness of the inability of the human to encompass the divine and a profound moral sense of both the tragedy and the wonder of human existence. He protests against tidy moral assumptions – as found in Utilitarianism, Kantianism and Situation Ethics. In *The Problem of Evil and the Problem of God*, Phillips develops the theme of the overwhelming evils that face mankind. His account of the Holocaust is especially moving, and his anger against any theodicy – such as that of Swinburne – which tries to justify God by reference to the utility of evil in the world is evident throughout the text. For Phillips, such accounts are *instrumental* uses of evil – evil as a means. But no one can justify torture because it might lead to some good: neither can we justify God in this way:

... I am opposed to instrumentalism in ethics. To rescue sufferings from degradation by employing cost–benefit analysis, is like rescuing a prostitute from degradation by telling her to charge higher fees.[3]

Key to his criticisms of inadequate theodicies is Chapter 3. Phillips lists ten morally insufficient reasons for evil, including opportunities for character development, logical necessity, acting as a spur to greater effort and to be better people, that things are not as bad as they seem, that suffering is never more than we can bear or that all will be redeemed after death. The flavour of Phillips' argument is evident in the following passage:

Swinburne's analysis leads to the vulgarization of the concept being analysed. It would make it possible for the Good Samaritan to say, on coming across the victim of the robbers, 'Thank you, God, for another opportunity to be responsible.' ... the sufferings of others are made instrumental to the self. Our moral growth is presented by Swinburne as the justification of those sufferings which he treats as the means of achieving it. We cannot speak of moral growth in this way ... Swinburne's instrumentalism worsens when he tries to justify the existence of horrendous evils, by saying that we need them in order to grow deeply in responding to them. Apparently, God knows this as well as we do, and wants to separate the men from the boys. ... But would the world not be better off without such attitudes to the suffering of others, attitudes that are a denial of the very moral concepts they claim to be elucidating? Here is a clear instance where a theodicy, in the very language it employs, actually adds to the evils it seeks to justify.[4]

Hick has responded to Phillips[5] by arguing that he pays too little attention to the frank admission of the problem of dysteleological evil, and by pointing out that he would never claim any justification of the Holocaust. He broadens his argument into a general critique of Phillips' entire philosophical approach, but seems not to address the key criticism of instrumentalism. Of course, Phillips' main target is Swinburne, but the general question is whether allowing actual suffering to individuals, especially when the suffering is so great, can ever be justified.

Exercises and Examination Advice

This chapter covers an area where there has traditionally been a great deal of confusion about what various philosophers have really said. A good starting exercise, therefore, would be to make a good summary of what Irenaeus and John Hick actually argue. It will also be worth taking the time to discuss the extent to which the idea of having a soul which needs to develop is a valid philosophical position.

Make sure that you have good summary notes on Irenaus and a clear understanding of his theodicy.

Then try these questions:

a. **Compare and contrast the theodicies of Irenaeus and Hick. [25]**

b. **To what extent is an idea of a soul needing to grow a valid philosophical position? [10]**

Notes

1. John Hick (1968) *Evil and the God of Love* (2nd edition; London: Collins Fontana), p. 331.
2. John Hick (1973) *Philosophy of Religion* (2nd edition; Englewood Cliffs: Prentice Hall), p. 43.
3. D. Z. Phillips (2004) *The Problem of Evil and the Problem of God* (London: SCM), p. 71.
4. *Ibid.* pp. 59–60.
5. John Hick (2007) 'D. Z. Phillips on God and evil', *Religious Studies* 43, December 2007, pp. 433–41.

The Challenge of Modern Science 12

Introduction

In this chapter we shall explore some of the views of scientists and philosophers on the creation and development of the universe. Building on the work you have already done on design, is there evidence of a divine agent responsible for the universe or is the universe and humanity itself the result of the forces of nature and blind chance? Was the watchmaker blind, as Richard Dawkins would have it? The more modern debate about intelligent design and irreducible complexity will be covered in the next chapter.

It is worth keeping in mind as you explore these areas that underlying the many debates is the question of humanity's place within this process. For example, it is arguable that much of the Roman Church's problem with Galileo was that he threatened the strongly held belief that humanity was the centre of the universe and therefore the reason for creation. It did not, of course, help his case that he was wrong about the orbits. He thought that orbits were circular rather than elliptical, which meant that any maps he produced would not help sailors navigate, unlike Ptolemy's maps which, based on careful observation, had been used successfully for centuries. Further, Galileo's telescope was not strong enough to make the observations which would demonstrate a heliocentric universe. It is worth recalling that Galileo was not tried because he contradicted religion but because his opinions flew in the face of the accepted science of the time. It is an error to cast this whole sad episode – for which Pope John Paul II apologized – as simply part of an inevitable war between science and religion. Taking the time to read about the trial of Galileo would be a good introduction to this debate.

Another trial which highlights the need to watch out for other agendas is the Scopes Monkey Trial in Tennessee in 1925. *Inherit the Wind*, a film of the trial, is well worth watching, making the case for science over religion in typical Hollywood manner. However, going beyond the evolutionary theory itself, the book Scopes was teaching from was using Darwin's theories to argue for eugenics as a way of improving the human race. The theory of eugenics – of scientific breeding – has mostly been discredited since use was made of these theories by the Nazis in the mid twentieth century.

Creationists and the Big Bang

There are not many people around today who do not accept the Big Bang theory of the beginning of the universe; though it is worth noting that there are some 'creationists' who argue for a literal interpretation of the Bible. If you think of the debate not as a strict dichotomy but as two ends of the same spectrum then you will see that you need to at least explore some of the views throughout the range.

Much like scientists, creationists come in all shapes and sizes, with a wide range of differing beliefs. It is worth knowing a few of these to understand the ins and outs of the debate. *Flat Earth* creationists would take a very literal view of the Genesis description of the world; namely that the earth is flat and covered with a firmament or solid dome. The way the writers of Genesis explain the waters in the vault above and below, for example, leads to a belief in the upper vault being the source of the Flood faced by Noah. While you may not meet many who hold this belief, the Flat Earth Society still exists and can be traced quite easily.

Another view is that of the *Young Earth* creationists, who hold that the age of the earth is between 6,000 and 10,000 years and that all life was created in six days, and by a day they mean 24 hours. The way of working the date of creation out would be to count the generations from Adam and Eve. Archbishop Ussher indeed tied it down to a particular date: he thought that creation began at nightfall preceding Sunday 23 October 4004 BC.

You may also want to explore the Omphalos argument, associated with Philip Gosse, which argues that the appearance of age was put into the world by God despite the earth actually being young. None of these, though, are the most common versions of creationism held today. It is generally accepted that *Progressive Creationism*, a form of *Old Earth* creationism, is the most popular view amongst modern creationists. A great deal of modern science can be incorporated into this position, with the Big Bang seen as evidence of the creative power of God. However, supporters of this would not hold with progressive evolution, believing rather that God created 'kinds' of organisms in the order seen in the fossil record and that newer 'kinds' were specially created, not mutated from earlier forms.

These are just a few of the creationist views, which you can explore in more depth, and while some may allow Dawkins and others to have fun ridiculing, it is worth remembering that the Big Bang theory itself is a theory and does not paint a complete picture of the universe itself. In fact, in many ways, for atheists the theory raises as many questions as it answers. As you have seen in your study of the design argument, it is not a good way to explain whether or not there is a divine agent behind our existence and the existence of the universe.

The theory argues that before the Big Bang there was nothing, no time and no space. Towards the end of the 1960s and the beginning of the 70s, three astrophysicists from Great Britain, George Ellis, Roger Penrose and, most famously, Stephen Hawking, looked at what Einstein's General Theory of Relativity would mean if it were extended to include measurements of time and space.[1] Their conclusions led them to argue that time and space had a finite beginning and that this beginning corresponded to the beginnings of matter and energy. This is not unlike the philosophical view of creation put forward by Boethius which you looked at earlier and which will be explored in more detail in the A2 book. For now you need to try to imagine the universe springing into existence from a singularity about 13.7 billion years ago. No one knows exactly what a singularity is, but they are believed to be zones of density found at the centre of black holes. At the centre of the black hole, finite matter is believed to be squashed into infinite density by the extraordinary gravitational forces. Infinite pressure on finite matter may make for some good debates with your friends who are studying mathematics and physics. Scientists do not know where this singularity came from, though they do seem to be clear that before this singularity nothing existed – no energy, no matter and, as I have said, no space–time continuum either.

As there was no space they had to conclude that the singularity did not appear in space but that space appeared inside the singularity. Science, then, cannot answer the question of where the universe came from, why it happened or even where it is. All scientists can really know is that we are inside it. Many say that Science is about how we came to be and that Philosophy is about why we came to be. Some argue that it is an oversimplification to divide arguments so crudely, as the two questions entail each other. As one philosopher argued, a 'why?' question can often be a 'how?' not yet answered. If we believe God made the universe, we do not just end the question as one settled. Why did he make it like this and not otherwise? How did a being purely spiritual bring about the material? I would hope that it is in this debate that scientists and philosophers recognize that they have much to learn from each other. It is also worth keeping in mind that examiners are not expecting anyone to find answers for these questions, but they will expect you to show that you have read around the area and that you understand what the issues are.

The Survival of the Fittest

Once you have worked through the 'how did it all start?' debate, you need to explore the arguments over the development of what some would call 'all God's creatures' and others the 'way DNA reproduces itself more effectively as time goes on'. Since most of this debate revolves around the implications of the work of Charles Darwin of Shrewsbury, England, you should know something about him. Charles Darwin was born on 12 February 1809 and died on 19 April 1882. This was a time of great change in Europe and Darwin's family embraced these changes. His grandfather Erasmus Darwin was philosophically radical, encouraging and writing about ideas which were found in the French Enlightenment, ideas about human equality and liberty, including, not surprisingly, ideas about the liberty to think freely about the existence of God and about natural origins for the earth's creatures.

Erasmus Darwin was an early member of an informal group of thinkers who called themselves the Lunar Society, a group that included James Watt, Joseph Priestley and Charles Darwin's other grandfather, Josiah Wedgwood. They would meet regularly in Birmingham to discuss everything from the latest philosophical and scientific ideas to the latest advances in technology and industry. It is therefore not surprising that Charles Darwin should also find himself pushing forward the ideas of natural philosophy.

It is well known that Darwin's five-year journey on HMS *Beagle* through a very wide range of the earth's environments set the course for the rest of his life. During the voyage Darwin made meticulous notes. His observations led him to the conclusion that a gradual transformation of species had taken place. This transformation had brought about the spectacular variety of life which now exists on our planet. So he had to come up with a theory which explained the causal features which had brought this about. He was also keen that the explanations were empirically verifiable.

The theory set out in *The Origin of Species* of 1859 can be seen as a series of causal elements that, working together, will produce the needed transformations. Scholars have summarized this process into nine sections.

1. Species are made up from individuals that change ever so slightly from each other in a wide number of traits.
2. Species on the whole increase in size over generations at an exponential speed.

3. Within a species, nature creates a situation where there is a constant battle for survival. This threat is brought about by things like predators, disease and limited resources.
4. Nature would seem to give some members of a species slight advantages over the others. These may allow some to resist disease better, others to be faster than their predators, or others to find their needs more easily.
5. It is then easier for these members of the species to survive and to care for their offspring.
6. As traits are inherited from parents, those who tend to survive better will pass on these survival traits to their offspring.
7. This is where Darwin gave the name of 'Natural Selection' to the process of passing on these favourable traits.
8. Eventually, over a long period of time, natural selection will tend to make the nature of a species change.
9. It is this process which ultimately brings about new species with different classifications. The processes also weeds out changes or mutations which do not strengthen life. This theory not only explains the variety of species but predicts the need for continued changes both positive and negative among species.

One of the advantages of this narrative for Darwin is that each stage is empirically verifiable. It is important when thinking about 'the survival of the fittest' – not Darwin's own phrase, but one given currency by his contemporary T. H. Huxley – not to think in terms of fitter meaning physically stronger. Carl Sagan, in his television series, *Cosmos*, gives a good example from Japan. Some of the crabs found near one of the islands had markings on their shells similar to a Samurai warrior's face mask. Superstition stopped the locals from eating these crabs, making that variation more likely to survive, and more crabs with these markings spread through the islands.

Once you have grasped the basics of these positions, it will be time to explore whether or not they support atheist or religious views of the nature of the universe and our place within it. Writers such as Richard Dawkins are very clearly on one side and you can see this from many of his writings such as this one in the *Guardian* on 9 February 2008. He describes the theory of natural selection thus:

Big enough to undermine the idea of creation but simple enough to be stated in a sentence, the theory of natural selection is a masterpiece.

Richard Dawkins (1941–), Professor of the Public Understanding of Science at the University of Oxford, has become one of the best-known critics of religion. He is noted both for the clarity of his writing and the vehemence of his views on faith. All his books are worth reading, and he has made important contributions to research in evolutionary biology. Among his books are *The Blind Watchmaker* (1986), *River out of Eden* (1995) – perhaps his finest work – and, more recently, his best-selling *The God Delusion* (2006). He is undoubtedly the best-known atheist in British public life.

Where he differs from previous well-known sceptics such as Bertrand Russell or A. J. Ayer is in the positivism he demonstrates about science. Russell and Ayer were both aware of the extent to which science is a set of theoretical constructs, with little certainty. Sir Karl Popper argued that the mark of genuine science is that it is highly *falsifiable* – that is, it is highly likely to be wrong. It is precisely because it might be wrong that it is so valuable. If I sought only certainty, I would have very little knowledge of any use. Consider the weather forecast: 'It will rain.' That is very likely to be true – somewhere, sometime it probably will. But if I say it will be raining in Glasgow at nine tomorrow morning, it will be far more useful to the citizens of Glasgow – and much more likely to be wrong, because it tells me far more. Dawkins's approach to science causes many in his own field – even when they are at one with his atheism – much discomfort. Science is cautious about certainty – that is why today's scientists prefer to talk of theories and principles rather than the 'laws' favoured by Enlightenment figures like Newton and Boyle. It is interesting that in *The God Delusion* he gives little consideration to such objections to his scientific assumptions. If scientific hypotheses are endlessly revisable, dogmatism becomes unhelpful, on both sides.

Other Darwinists, such as Michael Ruse, hold more nuanced positions and find Dawkins's evangelical atheism unhelpful to the debate. When reading Dawkins's discussions, Hugh's own students very quickly spotted the basic problem with this end of the debate; namely, most people with a modern sophisticated understanding of religion do not recognize as valid the extreme versions of religious belief that he criticizes. Father John Fitzgerald (1927–2007), a Carmelite monk who lectured in Philosophy at the University of Wales at Aberystwyth, was asked about Dawkins's views by an interviewer. His riposte was: 'If that is the kind of God you are telling me I believe in, I don't believe in him, either!' Father John's point was that Dawkins treats God as an alternative *scientific explanation*. As we saw in an earlier chapter, whatever kind of explanation God might be, it is not a scientific explanation in any recognizable sense. But we cannot go from saying that God is not a scientific explanation to the assumption that he is no explanation at all. There are plenty of good arguments on both sides without depending on fundamentalist approaches from either side.

Religious Responses

This debate is often presented as science and religion inevitably opposed. If a literal interpretation of Genesis is assumed, then of course a clash seems inevitable. But the history of the matter suggests otherwise. After all, the first edition of *The Origin of the*

Species was enthusiastically reviewed by a Catholic priest in the *Dublin Review*, and Frederick Temple, the future Archbishop of Canterbury (1821–1902), accepted evolution as established fact in his Bampton Lectures of 1884, published in 1885 as *The Relations between Religion and Science*.

In the twentieth century, the great palaeontologist (discoverer of Peking Man) and Jesuit, Pierre Teilhard de Chardin (1881–1955) attempted to articulate a vision of God in the world which not merely accepted evolution of the universe but placed it at the centre of God's purpose. Rather than saying simply that evolution and an expanding universe made no real difference to God's creation, Teilhard instead saw it as something which entailed the rethinking of the whole of God's purpose, not simply as a saving of souls but the working out of an intention for the whole of creation. Fundamentalists on both sides of the debate have tended to draw artificial battle lines in a very complex field.

Some religious responses, for example, would use the scientists' own language and start with the second law of thermodynamics, which is often better known as the scientific concept of entropy. This concept basically says that in any natural process there exists an inherent tendency towards the dissipation of useful energy, or in more basic terms, when left alone order tends to revert to chaos. This would seem to fly in the face of all you have just read about natural selection tending towards the improvement of those species most capable of survival. Many would see this as pointing towards a divine agent, particularly as the degree of chance needed for the creation of life is against all the odds. This point is best explored through a study of the anthropic principle.

There is also the obvious argument that many religious believers would use, which is that evolution can be seen as the method God uses to develop individual species within an overall plan beyond human comprehension. The same argument can be developed given a theist or deist view of a divine agent. A deist would simply see God as starting off creation and leaving it to develop – the sort of God who takes credit for the big picture but leaves the rest up to us. A theist can also see God in the developmental stages of each variation; though, given some of the dead-end mutations, such as the dimmer kind of dinosaur, one might need to question the nature of such a God.

There is no time here to go into all the arguments involved in this debate. However, I would strongly recommend that you do your best to read some of the writing of scholars such as John Polkinghorne, a scientist and a Christian minister who has written extensively on this area. He has, for example, a fascinating chapter on creation in his book *Science and Christian Belief*. Keith Ward also has several excellent arguments in his books and I would also recommend Alister McGrath's interesting little book *The Dawkins Delusion*.

It is important to remember that for those who do not depend on a fundamentalist, literalist view of sacred texts, Darwin did not undermine their faith. In fact it could be argued that he took the debate forward in the process of the struggle to understand God and the universe, a debate which has gone on for as long as human beings have asked questions.

It is just as important to make sure that you do not fall into the trap of looking for areas where scientists have no answer and saying, 'Ah, there is where the work of our God may be found.' That route only leads to the accusation of Peter Atkins, the Cambridge chemist and atheist, who said that 'finding God in the Big Bang is the last refuge of the desperate'. This route is often described as the 'God of the gaps'. The obvious problem is that as soon as a 'gap' is explained, the God you believe in becomes smaller. As our knowledge in this area is changing all the time, both scientifically and philosophically, the exciting thing is to research the writings and watch the latest television programmes and DVDs and come to your own conclusions. As I said earlier, evidence of research and reasoned evaluation is all that the examiners are looking for: there are no completely right answers in this area.

STRETCH AND CHALLENGE

One of the biggest changes in biology in the years to come will be through nanobiotechnology. Scientists will be able to make changes to human beings at the molecular level. As this technology develops, there may be profound changes in our understanding of what it means to be a human being. From a philosophical point of view it would certainly be a challenging exercise to ask what it would mean to be human in an age when such profound tinkering with humanity might be possible. Will we, for example, be faced with evidence that we are no more than the sum of our parts? Alternatively, there is already research which asks the question whether or not consciousness takes place at the quantum level. This would perhaps mean that awareness might still exist when all chemical and electrical activity in the brain has ceased. If consciousness turns out to be more than brain activity, it would be more than simply material. That would truly threaten any purely material explanation of our origin and motivation.

Exercises and Examination Advice

Make a list of the following terms in your notes and make sure you research them until you have a clear understanding of what each means:

Creationism

Big Bang Theory

Evolutionary Theory

Natural Selection

Survival of the fittest

It will also be important that you make good summary notes on the relevant writings of the following philosophers and thinkers:

Darwin

Polkinghorne

Alister McGrath

Dawkins

Hawking

As I have said several times now, it is very important that you are clear what different writers actually say. Sometimes books can give you the impression that beliefs such as Creationism have a simple interpretation and are therefore easily dismissed. If, however, you approach these ideas with an open mind, then you might well find that while many concepts are flawed, they are not easily dismissed and can contribute to our wider understanding: one of the great things about this whole debate is that, done properly, challenges to our belief systems can strengthen rather weaken these beliefs.

Also, when you explore the other side of the debate be aware, as you have seen above, that it is not the case that all Darwinians see the survival of the fittest as an argument against believing in a divine creator. This would be another good area to split into groups or into twos and research one side of the argument thoroughly and then have a debate in class. Those exploring science could, for example, look at Steady State Theory as well as the Big Bang and the various issues included in these studies. The other side could split into subgroups and argue for different versions of creationism.

Then you could try the following:

a. **Explain what the Big Bang Theory contributes to the debate about creation. [25]**

b. **'Science solves all the problems about where we come from.' Discuss. [10]**

Note

1. Steven Hawking and George F. R. Ellis (1968) 'The Cosmic Black-Body Radiation and the Existence of Singularities in our Universe', *Astrophysical Journal*, 152, pp. 25–36. Steven W. Hawking and Roger Penrose (1970) 'The Singularities of Gravitational Collapse and Cosmology', *Proceedings of the Royal Society of London*, Series A, 314, pp. 529–48.

Darwin's Black Box and Irreducible Complexity

Introduction

Before we begin looking at Darwin's Black Box, we need to be clear about the theory of intelligent design which would seem to be supported by this concept. Intelligent design seeks to postulate the view that certain features of the universe and of living things are best explained by an intelligent cause rather than a random process such as natural selection. In so far as one can say that Darwinism is an established and generally accepted view of the development of the universe, intelligent design can be said to be a direct challenge to the establishment.

It could be said that this group of scientists and philosophers are looking for evidence of design *qua* order and *qua* purpose in the universe, thus demonstrating the need for a designer. This search for design can be found in a number of scientific fields. In this chapter we are looking for evidence that certain biological data may lead to the inference that this data might point to an intelligent cause which can be tested or evaluated.

This might, in the years to come, be the most exciting and interesting part of the philosophy of religion course. The interface of science and religion is where the dialogue is crucial and most public and will be where the most significant questions about who we are and where the human race is going could be worked out. Science in many areas such as cosmology and nanotechnology seriously challenges humanity's understanding of where we fit into the universe and the extent to which we can change the way we develop physically and spiritually as human beings.

It is therefore important that you are careful not to fall for any version of the polemical arguments which take place between creationists on the one hand and those who would support Richard Dawkins on the other. When, for example, you look at intelligent design and the use made of this area by Michael Behe in his biochemical challenge to evolution, what he seems to be saying in the end is that in the same way as the laws of Newtonian mechanics do not work when one is describing the world of quantum particles, so evolutionary theory does not explain the biochemical processes which brought about the origin of life or which lead to processes such as blood clotting. Intelligent design and the search for irreducible complexity may lead some to a God or it may lead others to a search for new laws or explanations which are entirely part of the natural universe and need no outside agency.

Darwin's Black Box

So what is this mysterious black box which contributes so much to the intelligent design debate? Michael Behe and others have claimed that at the time of Darwin's theory, the cell was this black box. They are looking for biochemical machines within cells which have arguably not evolved. The key here is to understand that there would seem to be no evidence for the step by step process of evolution, examined in the last chapter. Instead Behe is arguing that the data of biochemistry within the cell leads to a belief in molecular machinery which is irreducibly complex. This idea is in response to a powerful statement Darwin made in *The Origin of Species*. Darwin said:

> If it could be demonstrated that any complex organ existed, which could not possibly have been formed by numerous, successive, slight modifications, my theory would absolutely break down. But I can find no such case.

The argument is that this case can now be found, thanks to electron microscopes letting scientists view what Behe describes as the Lilliputian land within our bodies. The point he is trying to make is that at this level there are actions taking place which are driven by machines that cannot be reduced to their constituent parts. In the past, Darwinian scientists pointed to a process in which they came together by making one slight modification, then another and another until we had added something useful to our cells.

Behe's most famous example is that of the cilium. In our bodies cilia can have two functions: one would be to help a free cell move about, the other to move fluid over the cell. In describing cilia he says:

> The function of the cilium is to be a motorised paddle. In order to achieve this function microtubules, nexin linkers, and motor proteins all have to be ordered in a precise function. They have to recognise each other intimately, and interact exactly. The function is not present if any of the components is missing. Furthermore, many more factors besides those listed are required to make the system useful for a living cell: the cilium has to be positioned in the right place, oriented correctly, and turned on or off according to the needs of the cell.

To make this idea clearer to the non-biologist, Behe makes a comparison with a mousetrap. To function properly a mousetrap needs to be built on a solid base and contain four other parts. It needs a hammer that clamps down on the mouse, a spring which gives the hammer the necessary power, a bar to hold the now energized hammer in position, and a catch to which the holding bar is secured, holding the hammer in coiled tension. Eventually, the jiggling action of a mouse, lured to the catch by a tasty piece of cheese, causes the holding bar to slip away from the catch, releasing the hammer to spring down upon the mouse. If any of the five parts of the mousetrap were to be taken away it would bring about the complete breakdown of its functionality. There would be no stability without the base, nor would the parts be able to keep the correct distance apart in order for them to work. If the spring or hammer were removed, there would be no way to catch the mouse. Finally, without both the catch and holding bar, setting a trap would be impossible. All the parts are essential for the machine to work. The implication of this is that it is impossible to build a mousetrap by Darwinian natural selection.

Behe asks us to imagine finding the following items in a garage: an old Popsicle (ice lolly) stick, a spring from an old wind-up clock, a piece of metal in the form of a crowbar, a darning needle and a bottle cap. While we could make these into a mousetrap with a great deal of work, they are not naturally suited for this purpose. For Behe the same will hold true for the cilium, which has analogous problems. He says:

> The mutated protein that accidentally stuck to microtubules would block their function as 'highways' for transport. A protein that indiscriminately bound microtubules together would disrupt the cell's shape – just as an erroneously placed cable that accidently pulled together girders supporting a building. A linker that strengthened microtubule bundles for structural supports would tend to make them inflexible, unlike the flexible linker nexin. An unregulated motor protein, freshly binding to microtubules, would push apart microtubules that should be close together. The incipient cilium would not be at the cell surface. If it were not at the cell surface, then internal beating would disrupt the cell; but even if it were at the cell surface, the number of motor proteins would probably not be enough to move the cilium . . . a hundred other difficulties would have to be overcome before an incipient cilium would be an improvement for the cell.

An Examination Perspective

If you were approaching an examination question on this area it would be best not to get too involved with scientific detail. We have tried to keep it to a minimum here, enough to try to keep to the integrity of Behe's argument without making it too confusing. This is just as important when looking at his critics. You will have seen in the earlier chapter on the Design argument the kind of critiques which were used to explore the work of philosophers such as Aquinas and Paley. You will also have noted the extent to which some of their arguments were genuinely refuted, while others were more often dismissed because of the ones which were refuted. Michael Behe, for example, points to how some of Paley's weaker arguments (which he calls the icing on the cake) were denied by scholars who often ignored the serious logical challenge that can be found in the watch example. It is important to be as careful with any critique of intelligent design.

There are many ways you could attempt to research criticisms of this form of the intelligent design argument. One may be to look at the flurry of writing over Behe's development of his work in his book, *The Edge of Evolution: The Search for the Limits of Darwinism*, published in 2007. On the one hand, Richard Dawkins tends to dismiss most of the work by pointing to other authorities, which ironically is something he is very critical of religious believers for doing. On the other hand, it does not take much of a search around the internet to discover the polemical arguments we are best advised to avoid; from the Dawkins Institute to the site dedicated to attacking the 'Darwinian Establishment', named the Discovery Institute, which lists ways that Dawkins is alleged to be wrong.

You should weigh the evidence for yourself, by critically reading as much of the debate as you can, keeping away from personal attacks as much as possible and looking for arguments that challenge the original thesis appropriately. This is part of the *thinking about* the issues which we discussed in the Introduction. So, for example, as an example of a straightforward criticism, we find Sean B. Carroll in his review, entitled 'God as Genetic Engineer', of Behe's book, *The Edge of Evolution*, writing:

> Behe's chief error is minimizing the power of natural selection to act cumulatively as traits or molecules evolve stepwise from one state to another via intermediates. Behe states correctly that in most species two adaptive mutations occurring instantaneously at two specific sites in one gene are very unlikely and that functional changes in proteins often involve two or more sites. But it is a non sequitur to leap to the conclusion, as Behe does, that such multiple-amino acid replacements therefore can't happen. Multiple replacements can accumulate when each single amino acid replacement affects performance, however slightly, because selection can act on each replacement individually and the changes can be made sequentially.

Those who choose to study AS Philosophy of Religion are rarely inclined towards science and may be saying, at this point, 'Please, enough of the biology.' While we have some sympathy with this position, we would encourage you to read as much of this debate as possible if you are to decide where you stand on the issue of intelligent design and the possibility of irreducible complexity.

In the examination, as has been said before, the examiners are not looking for your solution to this question; what you need to demonstrate is that you have seriously considered the academic issues involved and that you can justify whichever position you choose to hold.

We are not in this short chapter going to explore this whole area, nor begin to cover the many articles or books on the topic – we are merely opening up the discussion and pointing the way to more exploration. John Polkinghorne in *Science and Christian Belief* quotes a very useful statement by Charles Darwin in a letter to his friend Asa Grey, in 1860, the year after the publication of the *Origin of Species*. He wrote:

> I am inclined to look at everything as resulting from designed laws, with details, whether good or bad, left to the working out of what we may call chance. Not that this notion at all satisfies me. I feel most deeply that the whole subject is too profound for the human intellect.

Religious and scientific responses to the challenges of atheistic scientists to belief in a divine mind behind the universe should keep this thought of Darwin in mind. But it is not wise to jump from 'we do not know' to – 'it must be God'; lest we fall into the God of the Gaps fallacy which was generally abandoned in the twentieth century. It does not take much philosophical exploration to see that if your God fills the gaps, the more science explains, the smaller God becomes. However, it is equally important not to fall into the trap of saying that science can and will explain everything. Remember what we said about explanation in the second chapter on the Cosmological Argument. We may have to be open to the possibility for some things that there *is* no explanation, or that, as Dewi Phillips claimed, the existence of God is a *religious* quest, not a scientific one.

STRETCH AND CHALLENGE

At AS level you are generally not asked to go much beyond explaining the nature of the topic you have studied, demonstrating your understanding of the issues involved and the views of the relevant scholars. You would then evaluate a statement about the issue you are exploring. A way of going beyond that in this area of study and stretching yourself on this topic would be to bring in philosophical topics from earlier in the course and make comparisons. One way of doing this would be to look at the writings of Alister McGrath in his book, *The Dawkins Delusion*. The cover of McGrath's book quotes Michael Ruse, a confirmed Darwinian, as saying:

The God Delusion makes me embarrassed to be an atheist and McGrath shows why.

You could look at the idea put forward by Dawkins for the evolutionary development of religion and McGrath's response. He raises the question that if Dawkins wants to offer a Darwinian explanation of religion, – is he accounting for belief in God or for religiosity? McGrath says:

> The type of beliefs that might usefully be subjected to his sort of Darwinian explanation are what are sometimes referred to as 'hot cognitions', such as 'God likes me' or 'I am a sinner', which express felt meaning, rather than propositional statements such as 'God is good' or 'Jesus' mother was a virgin'.

Psychologists of religion are only beginning to understand the distinction between these 'hot cognitions' and affiliate group statements which may be given assent without being 'felt' to be true. So this leads McGrath to make a statement which may lead to some challenging discussion:

> People may be prepared to assent to propositional contradictions (renaming them 'paradoxes') and counterfactual belief statements (renaming them 'mysteries') precisely because the cognitive processing associated with their personal religion is not taking place at this level at all, but at an intuitive level that is not easily amenable to description in propositional terms.

This is moving from the evolution of the cell to that of the mind but it further opens up the debate on the extent to which evolutionary ideas are supportive of religion or complementary to religion, or are, as some would believe, the death knell for religions.

Exercise and Examination Advice

Make a list of the following terms in your notes and make sure you research them until you have a clear understanding of what each means:

Intelligent Design

Irreducible Complexity

Darwin's Black Box

Cilia

It will also be important that you make good summary notes on the relevant writings of the following philosophers and thinkers:

Behe

Dawkins

Darwin

Polkinghorne

Ward

As you will be aware, many modern scientists are working on the world of the minute. Significant advances are at the level of molecular engineering. This should, I hope, enliven any research you do into this question of whether at this level there is any evidence of design, let alone a divine designer. As ever, there is a wide range of views on the significance of these discoveries and you need to be clear about exactly which position is held by which philosopher or scientist.

You could, for example, do some research and work up a debate on whether or not something artificial such as a mousetrap can legitimately be compared with an organic machine such as a cilium.

You could then try the following:

a. Explain, using examples, what is meant by intelligent design. [25]

b. 'The intelligent design argument is no more than fundamentalist Christians seeing what they want to see.' Discuss. [10]

Appendix: Revision Notes

The notes here are not intended to be used as a substitute for your own course notes: they are a supplement, drawing attention to key points for revision.

Greek and Jewish Influences on the Philosophy of Religion

Ancient Greek Philosophy

Plato (427–347 BC)
The Soul:

- a simple substance, has no parts and is therefore indestructible
- has existed for all eternity and will exist for all eternity
- different from Christian conception where such a view would limit the power of God

- body is temporary and will decay
- true home is realm of the Forms, which we forget because of trauma of birth

Realm of the Forms:

- for all things there is an ideal form
- earthly things, such as chairs, merely copy these
- there are ideal forms such as individual numbers (oneness, twoness, etc., though not of 'number' as a general concept), truth, beauty and goodness
- the supreme form is the Form of the Good which enables us to know the others
- this world is an inferior copy (appearance) of the realm of the forms (reality)
- all learning is recollection of the realm of the forms, as is all discovery
- things in the realm of appearances are in a kind of ratio to things in the realm of the forms, so we can 'read off' by analogy. We need sun to see in the material world, so Form of Good is needed to understand in the Realm of Forms

Analogy of Cave:

- illustrates Doctrine of Forms
- shadows on wall represent shadows, images, illusions of this world
- prisoner released sees fire and objects – this material world
- undergoes painful introduction to better realm (enlightenment)
- first cannot look at bright things, only shadows (mathematical reasoning)
- then learns to look at objects themselves (forms)
- last of all at the sun (form of the good)

Aristotle (384–322 BC)
Rejection of Doctrine of Forms:

- Forms are incoherent – things are good in too many ways for there to be just one form
- Something is not more white by being eternal – whiteness and eternity are different
- No practical use: chairmaker learns by practice and study of chairs
- Third Man objection
- We learn through observation, not introspection

Body and Soul:

- Distinction between Form and Substance
- Substance is what the chair is made from; it is in the form of a chair
- Form is immanent, not transcendent – each chair is/has its own form
- Soul is the form/animating principle of the body
- When the body dies, so probably does the soul

The Four Causes:

- Material cause – what something is made from, such as wood
- Formal cause – the shape it has, e.g. of a chair
- Efficient cause – that which causes it to be, e.g. the chairmaker
- Final cause – its purpose, e.g. to provide a comfortable seat
- Aristotle's biology/world picture is teleological: things have a purpose

Prime Mover:

- Aristotle's God is indifferent to the world and co-eternal with it
- Spends eternity in the most Godly activity – contemplating his own endless perfection
- But is the Prime Mover, the cause of all motion and change
- Itself unmoved
- Fundamental to Aquinas' Cosmological Argument

Judaeo-Christian Influences on Religious Philosophy

God as Creator:

- God traditionally seen as creating *ex nihilo* though Genesis is not specific on this
- From beginning, God is seen as immanent and active in creation, delighting in it and relating to it
- God is omnipotent (all-powerful)
- Omniscient (all-knowing)
- Omnipresent (everywhere)
- If this is so, is he responsible for all that happens (e.g. evil)?

God as Good:

- Bible sees God as perfectly good and as giver of laws (e.g. to Moses)
- God seen as judge of human actions
- Raises question of theological voluntarism (Divine Command theory)

Traditional Arguments for the Existence of God

The Ontological Argument

- First devised by St Anselm (1033–1109) in *Proslogion*
- Argues that by definition God must exist (*a priori* argument)
- God is 'that than which nothing greater can be thought'
- If God did not exist he would not be 'that than which a greater cannot be thought' as a real God would be greater than an imaginary one
- So, to say God does not exist would be logically self-contradictory
- So, God must exist

- rejected by Gaunilo of Marmoutiers
- OA leads to absurd results if logic is applied elsewhere
- Anything would have to exist to be perfect
- A perfect island without existence would not be a perfect island
- Anselm replied that OA applies only to God
- Things like islands are contingent so cannot be necessary
- We may also ask whether concept of perfect island makes sense
- St Thomas Aquinas (1224/5–74) also rejected Anselm
- Things may be self-evident in two ways, in themselves or to us
- For something to be self-evident to us, we must be in a position to see the self-evidence
- We can only see God indirectly, through effects, so argument is closed to us

- Descartes (1596–1650) reformulated OA in *Meditations*
- God is by definition perfect
- Therefore God must have perfection of existence to be perfect
- Existence is a defining predicate (description) of the God concept just as having three sides is part of the definition of a triangle

- Rejected by Immanuel Kant (1724–1804)
- If existence is a predicate, there is no contradiction in rejecting a concept together with all its defining predicates
- Only contradictory if I try to keep God and reject the predicates or reject God but keep his predicates
- BUT existence is not a predicate as to say 'x exists' does not add a description to a concept but instead asserts that there is in the world an object corresponding to the concept 'x'
- Kant gives the example of 100 real and 100 imaginary *thalers*
- We could use example of a mermaid. The man who believes a mermaid exists and the man who does not are not disagreeing over whether the mermaid exists, only about whether in the real world there is something corresponding to the concept.

The Cosmological Argument

- First three ways of St Thomas Aquinas
- Rely on impossibility of infinite regress
- Motion: everything moved is moved by something else, we cannot go back infinitely, there must be an Unmoved Mover, who is God
- Cause: the same applies to causation: there must be an Uncaused First Cause
- Necessity and Contingency: everything around us is contingent (dependent on something else) so there must be a Necessary Being God to sustain the chains of contingency

- BUT cause and effect may just be our way of interpreting the world (David Hume 1711–76)
- 'Cause and effect' largely inexplicable. To say 'x causes y' may merely be 'whenever x, y'
- William Temple says an infinite regress may be unimaginable but it is not inconceivable. CA plays to limits of our imagination.

- F. C. Copleston appeals to Leibniz (1646–1716) – concept of sufficient reason
- Only God is sufficient explanation of the whole
- God is necessary existence

- BUT Bertrand Russell (1872–1970) argues that only propositions are necessary, not things
- Cites Hume to support notion that Copleston commits error of composition – because every human has a mother it does not follow the world has
- For Russell, the universe is just a 'brute fact'
- There may be no explanation

The Teleological Argument

- Aquinas' Fifth Way
- Nature, without intelligence, nevertheless is purposive (teleological)
- Therefore must be directed as an arrow by an archer

- Revived by William Paley (1743–1805) in *Natural Theology*
- Gives example of watch in wilderness

- From watch we must infer a watchmaker – from design in world we must infer a designer of all

- BUT Hume says in *Dialogues Concerning Religion* that the outcome of these arguments is determined by choice of analogy
- Is world any more like a machine than something natural but intricate like a cabbage?
- There are other ways to achieve apparent design – Epicurean thesis
- We cannot go from effect to cause greater than that needed to achieve effect (example of scales)
- World could be discarded effort of an infant deity or work of a committee
- John Stuart Mill (1806–73) points to amount of evil as pointing away from benevolent designer
- Evolutionary theory (Darwin) points to a random rather than an orderly, designed world – survival of fittest means if something doesn't fit it disappears; evolutionary history filled with waste and discards like the dodo
- Theory revived in modern times by Richard Swinburne, who argues that we should seek simplest and most economical explanation (Ockham's Razor), which is to say 'God made it'
- This is not a simple argument as all questions are then directed at God – why make it this way, etc.

The Moral Argument

- Fourth Way of St Thomas Aquinas
- Most associated with Kant
- Kant argues as a postulate of reason that goal of human reason is a combination of highest happiness and highest reason (*Summum bonum*)
- This is what we ought to achieve
- 'Ought' implies 'can'
- This is not achieved in this life
- Therefore it must be in the next
- We need God to provide this afterlife
- So God exists
- Questioned by Brian Davies – why a God to provide the afterlife?
- BUT seems to assume that source of moral awareness is God
- This is questionable: moral values could come from society, parents *et al.*
- Bioethics suggests there are good evolutionary reasons for values like altruism (Edmund O. Wilson, Peter Singer)
- Sigmund Freud supports this with alternative accounts of moral awareness such as Oedipus Complex inducing feelings of guilt

Challenges to Religious Belief

The Problem of Evil

- The classic problem outlined by Epicurus is the inconsistent triad:
- God is all-powerful and therefore could abolish evil;
- God is all-loving and therefore would wish to abolish evil
- But evil exists
- Therefore God is not all-powerful or not all-loving or both

- Two problems: moral evil, the harm humans knowingly do to others; non-moral evil (suffering, natural evil) from earthquakes, floods, disease, etc.

- Attempts to deal with evil and God called 'theodicies'
- Christianity rejects attempts to argue evil is not real

- St Augustine of Hippo (354–430) – soul-deciding theodicy
- Argues that God created everything good in its own way
- Evil is the going wrong of something itself made good (*privatio boni*)
- Evil caused by creatures rejecting God, first at Fall of Angels then at Fall of Adam and Eve
- Free will has real consequences in human suffering
- The fabric of the world went wrong because of these choices
- Hence natural evil
- We deserve to suffer because we were all seminally present in the loins of Adam
- Evil is either the consequence of sin or punishment for sin

- BUT raises the question of whether a perfectly good creation could go wrong
- Being omnipotent and all-knowing, God could foresee the evil and prevent it
- Presupposes very literal reading of Scripture
- Loins of Adam scientifically questionable – assumes homunculi
- God seems punitive

- St Irenaeus (c.130–c.202) – soul-making theodicy, further developed by John Hick (1922–)
- Believes this is a good world for soul-making involving challenges etc.
- Accepts free-will defence
- Real actions must have real consequences
- Earth is especially good for developing character, giving opportunities for virtues like courage, charity, patience, etc.

- Hick adds *epistemic distance* – God must leave us a space to be ourselves and to be genuinely free to choose him
- If God kept intervening to stop evil there would be no space for us to develop science and be genuinely free in relation to God
- God wants our love to be freely given
- Hick believes suffering can be justified by the joy of eternal love, which all may achieve – hell would be a place of temporary cleansing like Catholic notion of Purgatory

- BUT if all go to heaven why give free will in first place?
- God could give genuine choice of eternal life or extinction
- Does a loving father simply allow children invariably to suffer evil for the good it might do?

- Richard Swinburne suggests God puts evil into the fabric of the world to teach us the breadth of our capabilities
- God wants us to be great – true greatness involves ability to do great harm as well as great good
- God does not make a toy world for little people
- To those who suffer at the hands of others, Swinburne says they have one consolation – they are *of use* to others as moral opportunities: the worst human fate would be to be useless
- To these theodicies the central question has to be whether it speaks to the one who suffers – does the mother in the gas-chamber with her baby feel of use? How does God answer her?
- Hans Küng says God can only answer us by suffering as we do by the Crucifixion
- Process Theology uses idea of panentheism, in which all things are contained in God who is 'The Great Companion, the fellow-sufferer who understands' (Alfred North Whitehead)
- D. Z. Phillips attacks instrumental treatments of God – the man who falls among thieves between Jerusalem and Jericho is not there as a moral opportunity for the Good Samaritan. A loving father

does not leave children playing on the railway line as an opportunity for moral development. The consolation God gives us is as Love – the covenant that he is with us. 'Eternal Life' is not a temporal concept.

The Challenge of Modern Science

- The Science and Religion debate is not a simple dichotomy. Be very careful when reading anyone who thinks that it is.
- A study of creationism should show that there is no one simple theory. While the theories are often flawed we should face the challenges they present to us, using them to strengthen the debate and not just dismiss them out of hand.
- Some interpretations of Darwinism have raised significant questions for the argument from design. Be very clear about exactly what can be legitimately concluded from the theory about the survival of the fittest and what questions are still open to alternative interpretations.
- The Big Bang theory of the creation of the universe, while generally accepted today, still leaves questions about how it fits in with our understanding of how the universe works.
- The debate has been taken forward in recent years by the introduction of the concept of 'Intelligent Design'. Michael Behe has responded to the critics of his first book by looking more deeply for evidence of irreducible complexity.
- There remain serious questions about whether artificial machines are comparable with organic biochemical processes.
- Ultimately, as with many philosophical concepts, you need to explore whether or not the idea of Darwin's Black Box is justifiable or another kind of illusion created to justify belief in a particular kind of God.

Suggestions for Further Reading

This book is designed as an introductory text to the subject. It is not, and is not intended to be, a compendium of all that can be said or all that needs to be said on an endlessly fascinating subject. Good students will always read beyond their textbook, looking for new angles and opinions. What we hope to provide here is a guide to further sources, and the occasional health warning.

Internet Sources

On matters philosophical, the Stanford Encyclopedia of Philosophy (**http://plato. stanford.edu**) is most reliable, unlike certain entries in the popular *Wikipedia*. On religious matters, **www.newadvent.org** is very useful, not least because it contains a huge collection of translated texts, including the entire *Summa Theologicae*, and many classic texts of the Fathers of the Church. It also has the elderly, but interesting, *Catholic Encyclopedia.*

Other valuable resources

www.philofreligion.homestead.com/index.html
www.earlham.edu/~peters/philinks.htm#philosophers

These provide useful further links.

Background to Philosophy

It is important to have access to a sound encyclopedia of philosophy to ensure accuracy on key points. *The Oxford Companion to Philosophy*, the *Cambridge Dictionary of Philosophy* and the *Routledge Concise Encyclopedia of Philosophy* and *Routledge Shorter Encyclopedia of Philosophy* may all be confidently recommended.

For the history of Philosophy, F. C. Copleston's nine-volume *History of Philosophy* remains a superb resource. Bertrand Russell's *History of Western Philosophy* needs a health warning. It is excellent on the British Empiricists, but misleading and frequently downright wrong on those with whom he had little sympathy – including Aristotle and Aquinas. On Aquinas, Copleston's Penguin introduction remains excellent, and Brian Davies's *Aquinas* (Continuum) is a valuable modern source. A useful outline is *The History of Christian Thought* by Jonathan Hill (Lion).

Good anthologies are invaluable. Brian Davies has provided *Philosophy of Religion: A Guide and Anthology* (Oxford) and more contemporary readings may be found in Taliaferro and Griffiths' *Philosophy of Religion: An Anthology* (Blackwell). There is also much useful material in John G. Cottingham's excellent *Western Philosophy: An Anthology* (Blackwell).

Introductions to the Philosophy of Religion

There are several good and a number of suspect sources. A very sound text is Brian Davies, *An Introduction to the Philosophy of Religion* (Oxford). Still valuable, but over-priced, is John Hick, *Philosophy of Religion* (Prentice Hall). In more depth, Anthony O'Hear's *Experience, Explanation and Faith* (Gregg – pricey) raises a range of important questions in a readable style. Wide-ranging, thoughtful, and often very amusing, is T. J. Mawson's *Belief in God* (Oxford).

No one has done more than Peter Vardy to take the study of philosophy of religion into schools and colleges. There is much that is valuable in both *The Puzzle of God* (Fount) and *The Thinker's Guide to God* (with Julie Arliss – O Books), but they are marred by misleading material about realism and anti-realism. Peter Cole has also produced some helpful introductory material (Hodder). Surprisingly popular are books by Sarah Tyler and Gordon Reid. Although frequently very well presented, they contain major errors of philosophical understanding, and should be avoided.

Reading Further

The range of possible further reading is enormous. Some stimulating writers include Richard Swinburne (start with *Is There a God?* (Oxford)), Anthony Kenny (try *The Unknown God* (Continuum)), D. Z. Phillips (more difficult than some, but try Chapter 3 of *The Problem of Evil and the Problem of God* (SCM)), and Herbert McCabe (wonderfully elegant – try *God Matters*, *God Still Matters*, or *On Aquinas* (all Continuum)).

Read, explore, enjoy, reflect, and keep alive this most fascinating debate.

Index